String of Pearls

Mary C. Crowley

SECRETS OF
WISDOM AND FULFILLMENT

String of Pearls

WORD BOOKS
PUBLISHER
WACO, TEXAS

A DIVISION OF
WORD, INCORPORATED

STRING OF PEARLS: SECRETS OF WISDOM AND FULFILLMENT

Unless otherwise designated, Scripture quotations in this book are the author's paraphrase of the King James Version of the Bible.

Scripture quotations identified KJV are from the King James Version of the Bible.

Scripture quotations identified NASB are from *The New American Standard Bible*, © The Lockman Foundation 1960, 1962, 1971, 1972, 1973, 1975, 1977.

"Created in His Image" by William J. and Gloria Gaither. © Copyright 1969 by William J. Gaither. All rights reserved. Used by permission of Gaither Music Company.

"I Am Loved" by William J. and Gloria Gaither. © Copyright 1978 by William J. Gaither. All rights reserved. Used by permission of Gaither Music Company.

"For One Who Is Tired" from *Songs of Hope,* by Grace Noll Crowell. Copyright 1938 by Harper & Row, Publishers, Inc.; renewed 1966 by Grace Noll Crowell. Reprinted by permission of Harper & Row, Publishers, Inc.

Library of Congress Cataloging-in-Publication Data

Crowley, Mary C.
  String of pearls.

  1. Christian life—1960–   . I. Title.
BV4501.2.C77 1985   248.4   85–17994
ISBN 0–8499–0499–4

Printed in the United States of America

67898 FG 98765432

This book is lovingly dedicated to my family. Each morning when I wake up, I start each day by thanking God for the preservation of my family. And then I thank Him for my larger family —my church family and my business family. Without their love, loyalty, and prayers, I could not be where I am—or what I am—and this book could not be written. It is so wonderful to be loved.

Contents

Introduction

My hope in writing this book is to give my many friends and readers something to lift their spirits. I have included my favorite stories and truths—precious moments shared in many of my talks around the country throughout the years.

I know how busy people are, so I've created what I call a string of "pearls"—short chapters for quick reading that fit easily into the busy-ness of life. I hope that these words will tug at the heart strings, that they will awaken and challenge you with new ideas to put into action.

I believe it's always time to reach out and set new goals, to plan life's steps, to "reset the button" of our good intentions. So I offer a renewed challenge to live up to the opportunities that are given us—in our homes, in our work, and within our souls.

We live in a time when we need, more than ever, to immerse ourselves in a creative atmosphere of "upness." We need to read uplifting thoughts, to listen to tapes that have inspirational principles in them, to read things that keep us "thinking up." I play a lot of gospel music to keep me going all day. The Scriptures say, "Whatever things are true, whatever things are noble, whatever things are just, whatever things are pure, whatever things are lovely, whatever things are of good report, if there is any virtue and if there is anything praiseworthy—meditate on these things."

This book includes chapters on self-image, chapters on advancing on God's potential not limited by our own, on the principles of successful living, and on the many stages of life. And I pray that each piece here will be read or shared with someone so that God will lift them up.

I know so many people who think to themselves, "Oh, if I just had a different location, if I had a different body, if I had a different mind, if I had a different education . . . things would go better for me." I believe that in the final analysis we must learn the basic lesson of life: Under the sovereign hand of God, *If it is to be, it is up to me.* These ten two-letter words can change your life. Of course, they mean that you will have to have a feeling of self-worth, the knowledge that you can make things happen, and the understanding that God gave you a creative genius mind and expects you to use it.

Oh, life is no brief candle to me! It's some glowing torch which I've gotten hold of and which I must keep burning high and then someday pass on to the coming generations. This I feel about my work, my life, my kids, my grandkids, and all the people whose lives we touch and affect.

God help all of us to hold that torch high!

May God add his blessing to you, as I share these thoughts.

Mary C. Crowley

String *of* Pearls

1

Living Positively

LIVING POSITIVELY
IN A NEGATIVE WORLD

A beautiful crystal pitcher filled with water sits on a table just at eye level. It sparkles and diffracts the light of the afternoon sun.

You can change all that beauty with one small eye dropper. Add a single drop of ink to that crystal water and watch what happens.

You'll see a snakelike trail gradually make its way through the radiance. Finally the trail will dissolve. The pitcher no longer sparkles with clarity; its contents are foggy and dark.

It takes thirteen pitchers of water added to that original one to bring the water back to clarity again.

Our lives are like that pitcher. We have sparkling water to start with. Around us is negativism, defeatism, hatred, and despair. Naively, we think that "with a little bit of hope," we can keep our lives clear. But it takes thirteen times as much hope and encouragement—continuous hope and encouragement—to stay motivated and creative.

God never lets us down. But He never lets us off, either. He wants us to be everlastingly at work to keep the water of our lives crystal clear.

FIND AN
EVERLASTING
FRIEND

Through the years there's never been a time when I didn't know that Jesus loved me. I was born in Missouri, and when I was a year and a half old, my mother died shortly after my little brother's birth. I went to live with dear, godly grandparents, farming people—the kind of people who built this nation. Come Sunday, it wasn't a matter of asking, "Are we going to church?" Going to church was as natural as breathing.

We worshiped in our home. We praised God daily. And a blessing was always said at mealtime when we gathered around the dinnertable. My earliest recollection is of my grandparents kneeling at my bed at night praying for me. That gave me a wonderful heritage—that Jesus was my Friend. God wasn't off someplace ready to zap me down. I was important because He loved me.

Then one day my father moved to Washington state and married again, and I was picked up and taken rather unceremoniously across the country and dropped down in a rather hostile atmosphere. My stepmother did not know how to rear children or how to treat anyone with God's love. For seven years I lived in that atmosphere.

But with the heritage my grandparents had given me, I had the wonderful assurance that "Jesus loves me, this I know." Jesus became my mother, my father . . . just as He was my Friend. And I would go outside to walk in the tall piney woods of Washington and talk to Him as if He were right there, because He was.

When I was thirteen, I returned to live with my grandparents and committed my life to Jesus. I've disappointed Him many times, but He's never disappointed me. I know, just as I've always known, that He loves me and He's for me (Ps. 56:9). He also loves you.

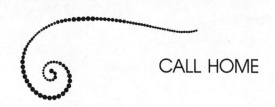

CALL HOME

In my business I've been in many homes, and sometimes I've heard mothers say to their children, "Don't act like that. God won't love you." When that happens, I slip over to the children and I say, "God would love you, but someone else might spank you."

You see, God loves us anyway—bad, good, whatever. He is the one Person who accepts us just as we are. That is a rare thing in this world—to be accepted just for ourselves.

So many times we look at people and try to decide, "Well, I wonder what her husband does?" or "I wonder who she is? What kind of car does she drive? Where does she live?" God accepts us just as we are.

It's reassuring to know that I can talk to God anytime. He's my real boss, and He's never out. He never says to me, "Now you're talking like a woman," and He never puts me down. In fact, I can "call Him collect" any time.

If I have a problem and I think I'll be up all night worrying about it, I just call God collect and tell Him about it instead. Sometimes when it's late at night, I tell myself, "He's going to be up all night anyway. So I might as well let Him handle it."

It's wonderful to know that God is my Father. God is your Father, too. Call Home! Call Home!

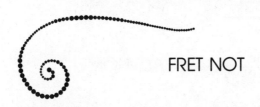

FRET NOT

Psalm 37: 1–5 is my pattern for living.

> Fret not . . . because of evil doers. . . . Trust in the
> Lord, and do good. . . . Delight . . . in the Lord; And
> He will give you the desires of your heart. Commit
> your way to the Lord, Trust also in Him, and He will
> do it (NASB).

Do not let someone else's sin rob you of your peace.

Fret not—because of what someone else is doing, and probably getting away with (temporarily, anyway). Trust in the Lord instead.

Oh, how I have had to learn to obey this commandment from God. How often we let someone else's sin rob us of our peace . . . But this scripture tells us to *trust in the Lord*—commit our way to Him—and He will take care of the situation, in His own way, in His own time.

Why is it so hard to surrender control of our lives to the Lord God Himself who made us, and knows us, and loves us?

2

His Likeness Is Mine

CREATED IN HIS IMAGE

"I advance in God's potential, not limited by my own!"

I heard Tim LaHaye say that once, and since then I have taken it as a theme for my life. In myself, I am not smart enough, good enough, bright enough, anything enough, to accomplish in my lifetime what God has accomplished—or what I have accomplished with His potential. When I advance with God's potential, not limited by my own, there is no limit to what He can do.

The apostle Paul said that he could do all things through Christ. And if anyone should have had guilt riding him to death, it was Paul. He had persecuted the Christians. He had killed them. He was a murderer.

I have thought so often about how he just turned all that over to God and moved forward with confidence and with such self-acceptance. He put all of his guilt on Jesus Christ who came to take away guilt.

Paul said something like, "I am the least. I am the worst . . . absolutely. I should have the worst kind of self-image, but I don't. I have the best because I am now a new creature. I can do all things through Christ—all things that are eternal."

I want to see everyone so steeped in God's potential that they never, never say, "I can't. I can't do that." Instead, they say, *"I can. Through Christ, I can!"*

Just think of what we can do with God's potential—it eliminates all the excuses, all the past problems, all our past history and everything else. We can perform to maximum ability—*and then some.*

Don't limit yourself by your ability. I don't ever have to be limited by Mary Crowley, and you don't have to be limited either. Get hold of what God's potential will do to you. Truly, the sky is the limit!

Advance with God's potential, not limited by your own.

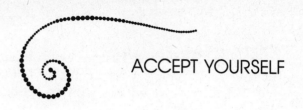

ACCEPT YOURSELF

Someone told me once that I was "cocky for Jesus."
I said, "Well, I guess you are right." A person with good self-acceptance will love and accept herself and go on from there. I love the song the Gaithers sing,

> I love—I am loved.
> Please take my hand.
> We are free to love each other,
> For the One who knows me best
> Loves me most.

Accept yourself. Love yourself. Jesus said, "Love your neighbor as yourself." He means we are free to love others.
I like the attitude of Psalm 100. Here's how it reads in the *New American Standard Bible:*

> Shout joyfully to the Lord, all the earth.
> Serve the Lord with gladness;
> Come before Him with joyful singing.
> Know that the Lord Himself is God;
> It is He who has made us, and not we ourselves;
> We are His people and the sheep of His pasture.
> Enter His gates with thanksgiving,
> And His courts with praise.
> Give thanks to Him; bless His name.
> For the Lord is good;
> His lovingkindness is everlasting,
> And His faithfulness to all generations.

If we read that every morning, it will do something to us! Shout joyfully. Serve with gladness. Come before Him with singing. Know the Lord. Enter His gates with thanksgiving and His courts with praise. Give thanks to Him and bless His name. Think of it, we are His workmanship! As another Gaither song says:

Created in His image, His likeness is mine.
Though conceived in earthly fashion,
    I've been born of the Divine.
There's no hill that I can't conquer,
    while I tread this earthly sod.
For I am made in the image . . . the image of God.

Think who you are and whose Image you were created in. Accept and love yourself in the light of that truth.

BUILD SELF-CONFIDENCE

In the Old Testament, Joshua told the people, "Don't let the trumpet have an uncertain sound." In other words, "Get in there and blow your trumpet with confidence!"

That makes me think of Justin Dart, who was chairman of the board at Dart Industries until his death a few years ago. When he was a young boy, Justin wanted a delivery job for a drugstore. He was so small that the man at the drugstore said to him, "Well, you are awfully little to be delivering for my drugstore."

Dart held his head high and said, "But I am a dependable guy!"

That kind of confidence got him the job, in spite of his size. And he went through life with that confidence and finally became head of Rexall Drug, which later became Dart Industries, a tremendous conglomerate industrial firm.

Justin Dart began his rise to success by saying, "I am a dependable guy!" His self-confidence caused someone to have confidence in him.

If we really believe something, we have to act as if it were so.

Remember God created you *To Be Somebody*. Accept His love, His redemption, His strength and make it your own. Blow your trumpet with a sure sound.

DO NOT LINGER
OVER FAILURES

Write this down somewhere in your Bible: *Do not linger over failures!*

We all fail. But we don't need to sit down and camp on those failures. We must get up and go on!

Just think of the apostle Paul. He could have lingered and mourned and beaten himself for years over what he had done before his conversion. We, too, might be tempted to give up, just thinking about our own failures. But God says, "If you have trusted me, I have taken all your guilt. Trust in me."

The guilt trip . . . so many people are in hospitals and institutions because of it. I think of a woman whose story was on the front page of the newspaper not long ago because she had written a book about her promiscuous life. She was sixty-four years old and was telling how many lovers she had had. She was almost bragging, but at the end of the article she made a very significant comment: "I know I shouldn't, but I still have guilt feelings." And I thought, *My dear, you are going to have guilt feelings until you turn them over to the Lord and change the direction of your life.*

You see, truth is written in the human heart. God said, "I will put My law within them, and on their hearts I will write it." And because His Ten Commandments are written within us, when we lie, something happens in our bodies and we feel guilty. This is why a lie detector works.

Guilt can drive people to despair. But we can learn to cope with guilt by confessing, repenting, and giving everything over to Jesus. As Corrie Ten Boom said, God "buries our sins in the depths of the sea and puts up a sign that says, 'No fishing!' "

No fishing! Let's not drag up our guilt again. Get up and go on!

YOU CAN NEVER HAVE
TOO MUCH JOY

Sometimes we are almost afraid to enjoy the peace of Christ because we are sure something will come crashing in and scatter that peace like a shattered pane of glass. People sometimes say that things are going so well they are sure something is going to happen.

Luis Palau talked about this attitude in his book *The Moment to Shout.* He was driving to the office and he heard a preacher on the radio discussing the fruits of the spirit—love, joy, peace, patience, kindness, goodness, faithfulness, gentleness, self-control. The Bible says, "Against such there is no law." Palau was waiting at the red light and the preacher said, "You know what that means. . . . It means there is no law against loving too much!"

Palau said he almost missed the green light.

The preacher added, "God will never come alongside you and say, 'You have loved enough. You'd better put the brakes on awhile.' There is no law against love!" Then he added, "You can never be too joyful in Jesus Christ. God is never going to say, 'You have had too much fun for a while, so now I'm going to cool it for you.' "

Jesus said, "Rejoice always." Too much of the time Christians are sour-apple people. We think being happy is superficial. But God says there is no law against joy. We can have as much of it as we want, if we allow the indwelling Christ to control us.

We can have it all . . . all the time. But we have to avoid thoughts like, "It has been peaceful for the last three weeks. Now it's time to worry a bit!"

God says, "Rejoice always, and again I say, rejoice!"

3

God's Game Plan

FINDING
GOD'S GAME PLAN

Some men die by shrapnel,
Some go down in flames,
Most men perish inch by inch,
Playing at little games.

Do you play at little games? I challenge you—have you searched out God's game plan for your life?

Many of you know football star Walter Payton, a running back with record-making yardage. I heard Walter speaking on television recently and someone asked for his definition of success—whether it was 100 yards gained in a football game.

His answer may surprise you. He said, "No. The measure of success for me is playing the game plan designed for that game to the very best of my ability. That is what I must do to feel good about myself—follow the game plan to the best of my ability."

Now that is a pretty good definition of the measure of success. You see, I believe God has a game plan for each life. I believe we will not really be successful until we find and play that game designed for us. We can't play a game designed for someone else. We have to play the game plan designed for us. If you are one of those who, as the poet puts it, "play at little games," I challenge you to search out God's game plan for your life.

A LOVING GOD
WILL MAKE A DIFFERENCE

Jesus told a parable about a man who had a large estate. One day he decided to leave for a while and go to a far country. Before leaving he called three servants to him; and he gave the first servant five talents, the next, two talents, and the third, one talent. Then after placing the money under their management, he went on his journey.

He was gone for a long time, and when he came back he called for an accounting. The first servant said he had invested the five talents and the money had doubled. The second said he also had doubled the two talents. To each, the master said, "Well done, good and faithful servant. Because you have been faithful over a few things, I will make you ruler over many. Enter into the joy of the Lord."

The third servant said, "Master, I knew that you were a hard man, and that you gathered where you had not sown and demanded where you had not given, and so I dug a hole in the ground and I buried the one talent. Here it is."

The master said, "Wicked and lazy servant!" And he ordered the talent to be taken away and had the servant banished into outer darkness. He said, "If you knew I was such a hard man, you should at least have put the talent into the bank where it would earn interest."

I used to think that was a harsh judgment. But I've read the story again and again, and I see that the third servant did not really know his master. He misjudged him as a harsh, demanding man, and acted accordingly. Isn't that how some of us see God? We think He is waiting to zap us if we make a mistake, and that He is hard and demanding.

That is the same mistake the servant made—misjudging the master, whom he didn't really know or love.

God is loving. God is fair. God is just. Trusting Him to be all those things will make such a difference in the way we make our choices. Our understanding of God influences our game plan, for God is our Father!

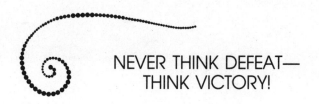

NEVER THINK DEFEAT—
THINK VICTORY!

Stick to the fight when you're hardest hit.
It's when things seem worst that you must not quit!

I learned that verse when I was a child, and it has stayed with me. You may give out, but don't give up. Never think defeat. Think victory.

Once I was privileged to have Corrie Ten Boom in my home for several weeks, and I remember her saying, "Look down on your problems from your position in victory in Jesus Christ."

She would say, "Jesus *was* victor. Jesus *is* victor. Jesus *will be* victor."

Those words still help me.

Roger Staubach, that wonderful, former quarterback for the Dallas Cowboys, also knows how to think victory. I've often said that Roger was never defeated—he just ran out of time! If you ever watched him play, you knew—right up to the last second—that he always played to win.

That's the way I think God wants us to live. There will be times when we feel beaten for the moment—but never really defeated.

I remember a game when the Washington Redskins played against the Dallas Cowboys. It was the last few minutes of the game and the Redskins were ahead by thirteen points. It was a Sunday afternoon and I had to take my oldest grandson to church for choir, so we dashed out to the car and turned on the radio to follow the game as we drove across town. Charlie Waters had been hurt and was in the booth as color commentator. The announcer Brad Sham said, "Well, there's just no way the Cowboys can pull this one out." But Charlie Waters said, "Oh, yeah? We're going to pull it out. We're going to win!"

In a little while the Cowboys got the ball and Roger threw a pass for a touchdown. But they were still six points short of victory. The Cowboys got the ball again with thirty seconds left and the announcer was already saying the Redskins had won. Charlie Waters said to him, "Man, you don't understand! We're a professional team. Ten seconds out there is like ten minutes to us."

Then Roger threw a pass for the last touchdown, and they kicked the extra point, and the Cowboys won the game.

I've thought about Charlie's words many times: "We're a professional team. Ten seconds to us is like ten minutes."

When we're down to ten seconds, do we panic, or are we professionals?

I've learned we must think victory. We plan, reason, and do our best—thinking victory all the time. That's how professionals win!

KEEP ON KEEPING ON!

My grandmother taught me not to "stop at the first tired."
I've seen lots of people who "stop at the first tired."
They get weary, and so they quit. But if you keep on keeping on, you know you'll get a second wind, and then a third or a fourth wind. You really *can* keep going.

We had a seminar one time for our women at Home Interiors, and the slogan was "Do your best. Give your best . . . and then some."

And then some. . . . Keep on keeping on.

You'll be amazed at what else you can do. We need a challenge that pulls out the best in us. After a while, even our best will increase.

Keep on! Let's do our best . . . and then some.

In an exercise class I recently attended, the instructor said, "If you get tired, stop—but don't quit. Take a moment to get a little rest for a breather and then get back into the rhythm of the exercise."

If you get tired—and you will—you may have to stop a moment. But don't quit. "You may give out . . . but don't give up!"

4

Choices

YOU HAVE THE FREEDOM TO SET YOUR GOAL

A goal is the target of behavior. I have a little saying I use all the time: "You have the freedom to make the choice; but after you choose, that choice controls the chooser."

Let me say that again in terms of life's goals: You have the freedom to set your goal, but after you set it, the goal controls the chooser and the choices you make.

First, you make a choice. You choose to do with your life what *you* choose to do with it. After that, your choice will control you.

I've seen people set a goal to make a lot of money, and they've achieved the goal. But that goal controlled them completely, and often their victory was empty and hollow.

We must wait upon the Lord very strictly for direction— wait for what He wants us to do. Choices are serious. Of course, waiting doesn't mean a "sitting around" kind of waiting. I like the saying, "Sitting and waiting won't put fish upon the plate. The Lord provides the fishing. We have to dig the bait." We have to *do* something.

As I've said so often, *"If it is to be, it is up to me,"* under the sovereignty of God.

We have choices. We have the freedom to make them. And we have the privilege to wait upon the Lord.

Grandmother always said that the Lord reserved the *best* for those who leave the choice to Him.

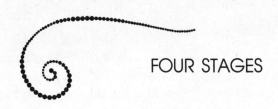

FOUR STAGES

Every institution, every company, every agency, every church, and every life is lived in one of four stages.

The first stage is the creative stage. It's a stage similar to what happens when we first became a Christian. We were excited, enthusiastic, and we wanted to study the Word and get to know God better. That same enthusiasm occurs in a business, a church, or an institution. The creative juices are just flowing! Everybody is at work—visiting, going to see people, building the business. It is an exciting time, and obstacles are only to be overcome. Our enthusiasm brings excitement to everyone else. There is zest and pride in each other and momentum!

When things begin to go very well, the second stage may begin, so we have to be very careful. *That second stage is the management stage.* I've seen many businesses in this management stage. Their priorities center on such things as who has a name on a parking space. The early enthusiasm is lost and they've entered a "comfort zone," where they begin to forget the excitement and design programs and manuals. Time is spent in the office more than out with people. For Christians, Bible study can become just a habit, if it is even that. Church-going can become a ritual. Religion is the "order of the day" instead of a relationship. Programs replace people as a priority.

We have to be very careful here, because we may soon get into the third stage unless we find a way to return to the first stage. *The third stage is the defensive stage.* It's amazing how we can defend what we do. The Proverbs say we can rationalize our activities and our behavior . . . but is the Lord convinced? We strongly defend our lack of personal growth and our lack of institutional growth.

I've found this defensiveness at work in sales and in business. I try to train someone who is defensive and they say, "Yes, but. . . ." I can't get through to them because they are on the defensive.

Anytime you begin to defend your actions, watch out! Remember what stage you're in, because if you don't come back to stage one—that creative, exciting, wonderful stage— you may find yourself in stage four which is next door to "bankruptcy."

Stage four is the blaming stage. You blame your family, your heritage. You blame your lack of opportunities, money, or time. You blame the economy, teachers—everybody but yourself.

Taking responsibility for our own actions is one of the marks of maturity. We must be responsible human beings.

We must get back to stage one. A doctor I know has a sign on his desk which says, "There is not much wrong with people that can't be cured by a little excitement."

Let's never lose the wonder of it all!

ALL TRUTH IS NARROW

The other day I read in the Washington *Times* that some-body thought Pat Boone was "narrow." Dr. Criswell, my pastor, likes to say that "all truth is narrow." Scientific truth is narrow. Mathematic truth is narrow. Geographic truth is narrow.

If you have a note due at the bank, you will probably work hard to pay it off. If you owe a thousand dollars you can't go to the bank with nine hundred dollars and say, "I want to pay off my loan." The banker will say, "That isn't enough." And you might say, "Oh, how narrow. How narrow-minded you are. I'm more liberal than that. You know, I have a broad mind!" That kind of talk doesn't change the fact that you owe a thousand dollars.

We had some very cold weather in Dallas recently and the ponds froze over. On one of those cold days, you couldn't say, "I'm going to take a swim in this pond." Some-one would say, "You can't do that. It's frozen over." You wouldn't say to that person, "Oh, how narrow you are!" Water freezes at 32 degrees. That's how narrow truth is.

When we wait upon the Lord for direction for our lives, we are seeking the truth. God's truth will set us free, Christ says. The truth which sets us free is narrow—it is exact and true and trustworthy. Water freezes at 32 degrees and a thousand dollars is always a thousand dollars. We can count on what Dr. Francis Schaeffer calls *"true* TRUTH."

5

Blessings, Achievements, and Goals

COUNT YOUR BLESSINGS

Most of us have bags of some kind for carrying money, books, a comb and brush. But I like to think of a bag—spelled B-A-G—as Blessings, Achievements, and Goals. "B" helps me count the BLESSINGS God has given me.

Yes, we should count our blessings. Angels will attend! It's so easy to forget those blessings. It's easiest to remember them in the spring when the sun is shining and the bluebonnets are beautiful on the hillsides. But when school is out and we need a job, and we get a lot of turn-downs or "I'll call you" responses, we begin to lose the joy of counting our blessings.

In Home Interiors, we offer a lot of seminars where people have to stand in line for their breakfast or lunch. We often have five thousand people waiting for a meal. We have to remind them that it is better to stand in this line than in the unemployment line!

In all circumstances, we need to count our blessings!

We have a mind; God gave us enough creative genius to do anything. And we have opportunity; we live in America.

When you wake up in the morning and you have something to do, someone to love, health to keep you going— you are blessed!

Go for it one day at a time

REMEMBER YOUR ACHIEVEMENTS

B-A-G also helps me remember to look for strengths instead of weaknesses. The letter "A" stands for ACHIEVEMENTS. These are the things we have already accomplished. Some days we have a difficult time; someone may have put us down or rejected us for some reason. But we should keep right on in the same direction.

Sometimes interviewers ask me, "Well, haven't you ever been discriminated against as a woman in business?" I say to them, "Maybe I have . . . I just didn't have sense enough to know it!" I always figure that anybody who tries to put me down diminishes himself or herself, and not me.

You see, I believe that everybody is *somebody,* and I always feel sorry for the person who is trying to put others down. I prefer to look at achievements. We can all do that— we can look back and see how far we have come from where we started. We must build on our strengths, not our weaknesses.

If I had any advice to give about achievement it is this: Get your mind off your mistakes and onto your accomplishments. Think of them over and over.

If someone tries to tell you how stupid and dumb you are, just write it off as *part* of an accomplishment, and not the main part. They are not talking about *you* as a person, but only about one day when you goofed badly. Don't dwell on it. Remember your strengths, and never forget them.

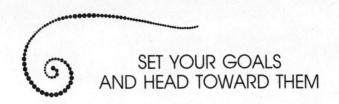

SET YOUR GOALS
AND HEAD TOWARD THEM

The letter "G" in B-A-G stands for GOALS.

You can't go anywhere without goals. I don't know how people live without them. We are goal-oriented people. God made us that way. He wants us to have a vision, and His Word says, "Where there is no vision, the people perish" (KJV).

A vision is a goal. Sometimes it's just a goal of getting through the day. Once I had a group of young people in my home and I asked them about their goals. One of them had a magnificent goal. He wanted to be a doctor. But another one said, "I just want to pass!" That was his immediate goal. And it was an important one at that moment.

Whether your goals are immediate or long-range, have some goals. Re-do in your life whatever must be changed in order to reach those goals. Re-do your thinking, your attitudes, your directions.

Renew. Review. Re-do. That is my advice for setting and reaching goals. Remember how everlastingly important you are, and set worthy goals!

6

Be Glad You're a Woman

WHAT DO WOMEN WANT?

I believe women are special. For forty years I've worked with thousands of women in sales organizations, and I've learned their characteristics from talking with them and walking closely with them. I've heard men say, "What do women really want?" and although I'm not a psychologist, I believe I have earned a Ph.D. in experience. Through the years I have learned that women want three things:

First, they want *to be accepted.* "God created them male and female," the Bible says. Women want to be regarded as equal in God's sight and to be viewed as intelligent human beings. If you study the Scriptures, you will find no place where God does not accept women in that way, regarding them with equality, intelligence and value.

Second, women want *to be loved and understood.* I've heard men say, "There's no way you can understand a woman!" That's right, in the same way that no woman can completely understand a man. Yet women want to be loved for themselves, and they want the men in their lives to try to understand where they are "coming from," what they are think-ing, what their goals and desires are. If they can't be under-stood, they at least want to be loved.

Third, women want *to be needed and developed.* I think one of the reasons the feminist movement took root and made headlines is that women did not feel they were needed, or that their talents were being developed. They were treated as a trophy in a man's showcase, a gem in his home, a special thing of beauty, or a sign of the man's ability to attract beautiful women; or else they were treated as a drudge (whether a scrubber of floors, or the homemaker of a fine home). They were treated as a lesser person and their work regarded as lesser in value than the husband's work.

Women need a balance. They need to *feel equal,* to *feel loved and understood,* to *feel developed.* They must feel that their work as a homemaker and mother is vital to the mar-riage and equal in value to the bread-winning role of the husband.

The husband-father must recognize the hard work of managing the house and doing the housework. He can offer appreciation, recognition, and romance to this woman who makes his home—she really is the Queen of the home.

With so many women entering the work force and still having to manage the home and do all those other things, the tremendous stress is hurting both wife and husband. God help us all to recognize the value of our contributions to each other and help us to support each other.

GENESIS ACCORDING TO MARY

When God created the world in "Genesis according to Mary," He looked at it and He said, "That's good."

Then He created man and He said, "That's good, but I believe I can beat that."

And then He made woman!

He made her with a distinctiveness, an intuitiveness, a sensitivity to the needs of others. He made her aware of the beauty around her. He caused her to bring an element of beauty and romance into the world that would not otherwise be there.

I believe God designed women to be the inspiration of mankind.

I drink from a full cup. I am deeply glad to be a woman. I'm thankful for God's creativity in making us distinctively different and individual.

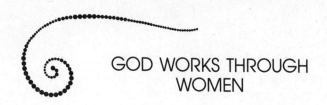

GOD WORKS THROUGH
WOMEN

As I grew up, I learned to take my models from the Bible. In the Old Testament my model has always been Deborah.

I once asked a group of thirteen hundred preachers in Memphis, "Who was Mrs. Lappidoth?" They didn't recognize the name of this woman of the Bible. That's because God always called her by her own name—Deborah (see Judges 4).

God knows our names. He never mistakes us for any other person. He has a plan for us and a job for each one of us.

Deborah discovered God's unusual plan for her life, and she never wavered from trusting God once she discovered it. She was a judge during the days when her people were oppressed by the king of Canaan. They came to her with all their problems.

She never said, "What can *I* do? I'm only a woman!" She was known to be wise and compassionate in the ways of Almighty God.

She went to Him in prayer for her people, and one day His answer came in a startling way.

She was led to call Barak, the little commander-in-chief of the rag-tag army of Israel. She said, "Has not the Lord God commanded you to mobilize ten thousand men and go up to Mount Tabor, and he would deliver Sisera into your hands?" Sisera was the wicked military commander of the nation that oppressed them.

Barak's answer was surprising. He said to Deborah, "I will go—if *you* will go with me!"

Barak was no different from men today. He needed

encouragement. I believe God created women to be the inspirers of mankind. We are the motivators of action.

Deborah agreed to go, but only on one condition—that Barak would take no credit for the battle.

So Barak began rallying his army, fearing the army of Sisera who had nine hundred chariots of iron while he had none. He had no weapons for his army, either. He seemed to forget that "one plus God is a majority." He was dragging his feet.

Deborah finally came to him one day and said, "Up! This is the day. The Lord God has gone out before you."

The victory was won that day, and the people sang a song of praise. The Bible tells us that God's people had rest and peace for forty years—because one woman believed and acted on her belief. And I thought, Lord, if you could do that through Deborah, I wonder what you can do through Mary C. Crowley? And I signed up to find out!

Today I would like to say to you and to me and to all of us, "Up! For this is the day. The Lord God has gone out before us!" We may think we are pioneers, paving new ways. But God has gone out before us! We are never alone in our ventures.

A MODEL
OF HOSPITALITY
AND HARD WORK

I was forty-two years old when I started my business. My model for my work has always been Lydia, the seller of purple in the New Testament.

When Paul and his troops came to the continent of Europe to begin their witness they wanted to find some praying people with whom to worship. They asked for directions and they were told of a group of women praying down by the river.

(I've found that women are generally better pray-ers than men. Perhaps that's because we have men to pray over. Raising my son—who had lots of creative imagination and who now works beside me at Home Interiors—brought me regularly to prayer. I finally prayed, "Lord, he's going to do something great; please make it legal!")

Seeking these praying women, Paul went down to the river and found Lydia and the others. She welcomed him and gladly heard the gospel. With her household she accepted Christ that day and worshiped God. The Bible tells us how she offered her hospitality to Paul and his team.

Lydia was a business person. A professional. A sales person. She was successful and hospitable. I believe she was one of those people who beautified whatever she touched.

When we started Home Interiors, we hoped to bring that same hospitality into the homes of America. We wanted to give women an opportunity to use their creative genius. We wanted them to work from home while their children were small. We think we invented "flex-time" long before the government thought of it. And we found that our idea worked beyond anything we could have imagined.

I believe God blessed our idea because we sought to honor Him in our homes, our lives, and our work and because we sought to serve and bless others.

7

Attention, Attention

ANSWER THE FIRST TUG

Five o'clock . . . the end of a busy day, and also the beginning. You stand in a familiar place—the kitchen. Supper is underway, and the telephone rings. An urgent caller reminds you of something you must do in the morning. You hold the phone with one hand, stir the sauce you are making with the other, and then you feel a sudden tug at your skirt. You have no free hand to reach down and touch the touseled head that rubs against you for attention. You are almost too tired to make the effort. Yet it is something you must do.

On other days—which you have vowed never to repeat—annoyed by the unceasing tug on your skirt, you have ended your phone conversation in hasty exasperation, and without looking up from the contents of pan in front of you, you've snapped "What do you want?" and kept on stirring. On those days the little hand stopped tugging, the face looked up at you in disappointment—a magic moment was lost.

Today you vow to do better. You look this little child in the face as he tugs so desperately for your attention. You have learned that one reassuring smile will do it all.

48

"I'll be with you in exactly three minutes," you say.

His face relaxes. You have recognized him as a person. You have acknowledged his need for attention. And you have given yourself three minutes to finish the phone conversation, stir and season the dinner, and then give your child that coveted attention.

Everything has been preserved by that three-minute promise—your child's personhood, your own disposition, and that precious chance to communicate.

How important it is to answer that first tug!

WE ALL NEED ATTENTION

Your watch says 2:03 P.M. and you were due at an appointment three minutes ago. The traffic light ahead is red, you hit the brake and look down at your feet. An ugly run in your hose has started from your toe toward your ankle, and it is likely to keep on moving upward.

You can't appear at your appointment—late or not—looking like that.

You pull quickly into a parking lot and rush into the nearest department store, trying to be calm. The hosiery department is close to the door, but it is crowded with midday shoppers. You quickly select "medium, tan, seamless," in your favorite brand, and you head for the checkout counter.

Three people stand ahead of you, and two others are trying to get the cashier's attention. It's just your luck that a sale is underway. You try one end of the counter, then the other, dancing back and forth to show you are in a hurry. You hope the clerk will catch you out of the corner of her eye.

She does. She frowns a little at first. You can see her job is difficult today . . . too many people and not enough help. But she knows what to do. She looks right at you, across the heads of the people in front of you.

"I'll be with you in just a moment," she says. Somehow, she understands. She has seen you, recognized you as a person, and put you at ease.

Her small act of courtesy and concern says she knows your time is valuable. She takes you seriously.

How much more important we feel when someone like

this checkout clerk recognizes us and takes a moment to let us know it. We all need attention!

Another day, in another place, we can return the kindness to someone else.

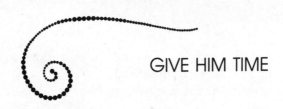

GIVE HIM TIME

Here's a scene that may have happened in your home—especially if you're a full-time homemaker.

You've been home all day, while your husband has been out in the workaday world. You've been planning meals and budgets, cleaning, keeping up with the laundry, running that taxi service back and forth to school, music lessons, ball games—and the list doesn't stop there. When your husband comes home, you're preoccupied with all that busy-ness. You're so involved, he feels that other things are more important to you than he is.

He needs attention, too. When he comes in the door, give him at least thirty minutes of personal attention. Offer him a glass of iced tea or a cup of coffee, then sit down with him and find out how his day has been. Then he'll usually go on into the den and watch television—or go out in the backyard or garage and work on something. *He's had his moment of attention.*

I know this is hard sometimes. As women, we often think, *I need attention too.* But there's a timing to attention. I think our needs come after the evening meal. Maybe he'll say to you, "Sit here and relax awhile; the kids and I will clear the table." Or maybe you'll have to help him remember your needs. If the kids are big enough, perhaps you can tell *them* to clear the table, and the two of you can sit by the fire or sit on the back porch or take a walk. That's his time with you, and maybe he will thank you for a good meal, or recognize your fantastic managerial ability, or just listen to you for a while.

It's so important that each one in the family learn to give *attention* at the *right time.* Wouldn't it be wonderful if every day each mate would ask the other, "What can I do to make your life happier today?"

8

Giving Is a Blessing

TWO SILVER SHOVELS

A silversmith in England made me two silver shovels—a tiny one and a larger one, and I often wear them on a silver chain. They were brought to me by a young man we sponsored through college and seminary. He is now teaching in South Africa. His brother-in-law made the shovels for me at his request.

They symbolize a story he told me about a philanthropist who was once asked, "How can you give away so much and have so much left?"

The man replied, "I don't know. I guess it happens like this: I shovel it out, and God shovels it in, and *He has the bigger shovel!*"

God invented giving. He has all the resources. I've found that you can never outgive God.

GRATITUDE COMES LATER

I was honored recently with a wonderful letter from my son. I will treasure it more than any gift in all the world. I share it here so you can see how much more is "caught" than "taught" in raising our families:

Dear Mom,

On this special night in Los Angeles, as you are honored with the Jubilate Christian Achievement Award, I'm reminded of the many honors you've brought your children and grandchildren. As your only son, I speak from the past and present as I see how far you've come in your life, both financially and spiritually.

I remember when you were a bookkeeper working to support your two children, and you were faithfully tithing every week. Oh, how I thought my mom would starve us to death in keeping her commitments to the Lord! But I'm thankful that you believe strongly in your faith and that you've kept your commitment.

There was the time when we purchased our first new chair, when we lived on Summit Street in Dallas. We paid fifty dollars for that chair at the time and we didn't have a car, and we were walking or taking the bus everywhere. I knew where we could have bought an old car for fifty dollars. We could have fixed it up with the money you were tithing to the church. Oh, how I thought we needed that car. I'm glad that you set an example and held to your faith and discipled us as you were raising your son and daughter.

Then you started selling Stanley Home Products and

needed a car to do the business, so we were able to stop riding the bus. We all pitched in to help unpack your freight and get your orders ready. You taught your children how to sell and to give service and at the same time add a little love to others' lives.

Then came the more glamorized selling of gifts, and you took that big step and ventured into your business with your family and friends for encouragement and financial support. From the beginning, you had faith and determination that the business was going to succeed.

In the lean years we learned that nothing comes easy, and there's a price to pay for success. Mom, as long as I can remember, you've done nothing without having God in it first. One must learn to evaluate and set priorities, and you did this. In those times of your faithfulness, I believe Jesus Christ gave you a special blessing. You have all of our heavenly creation, wisdom and insight given by God, and the joy in life that cannot be measured.

I'm very proud of you. You are indeed a super mom.

With love,
Your son,
Don Carter

You can see why that letter means so much to me. It tells me how important it is for us to stick to our beliefs and live them out—with God's help.

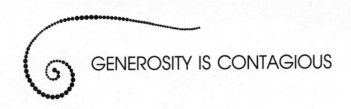

GENEROSITY IS CONTAGIOUS

Do you know something about generosity? It's contagious.

I think people aren't generous because they haven't seen a lot of generosity. If they were to see it at work among God's people, they would catch the spirit of generosity and start an epidemic. But you can't catch something that hasn't been given out.

If all God's people would literally believe in and practice tithing, who knows what would happen?

It's really very simple. The spirit of giving is like fire. It spreads faster and faster, once we let it catch on. But we must each do our part—we must trust God and tithe. And, as Scripture says, God will open the windows of heaven and pour out blessing until there is no more need.

May you catch the irresistible spirit of God's generosity.

ASK GOD TO HELP YOU GIVE

People sometimes say to me, "Well, if I had as much money as you do, I would give too."

I answer, "How much do you give of what you have? That's the secret."

I don't know where I got it, but God endowed me with the love of giving. I'm so grateful because He gave to me—everything He had. When I learned to tithe many years ago, I didn't have any money. I simply had to take the first step and be willing to give.

I think of the fellow who came to the Lord in faith as he was building up a business. He asked his pastor to pray with him. "Pastor," he said, "I want you to kneel here with me and pray God's blessings on this business I'm starting. I will promise to give God a tenth of my income."

The pastor bowed and dutifully prayed that God would bless the business, and indeed it grew and grew so that pretty soon there was a tremendous amount of money coming in. That meant the tithe was a very large sum.

Feeling uncomfortable about giving away so much money, the man went back to his pastor and said, "Somehow, I want you to ask God to relieve me from my promise to give 10 percent. It's just too much."

So the pastor knelt down and prayed that God would diminish his business and make it poor again.

"Oh, no," said the man. "I didn't want that."

"But that's what you asked for," said the pastor. "Giving and receiving from God are in proportion, and you have to understand that principle. God doesn't give money to people when He can't receive it back through people. Money must pass through us to God."

Success is not an achievement to be enjoyed and hoarded. It is a trust to be administered in a spirit of giving.

HANDLING CRITICISM

My grandmother told me once that if you're doing anything worthwhile, you'll have criticism.

Criticism—to a person doing a job—is like bullets to a soldier. If he's told to take a hill, he can't say, "But I can't go up that hill. They're shootin' bullets at me." He has to go up the hill.

If you're doing something worthwhile, do it and never mind the criticism. If you're right about what you're doing, time is on your side. Beware . . . don't let the media or anyone else set your agenda for you. If you're on track, you can ignore criticism or pressure. But you must beware of your own actions. Don't go out and invoke criticism by doing foolish things and presenting a foolish image.

If you know your goals, if you know what you're supposed to do, you needn't be concerned about the fellow next to you, or the guy in the next office who has another idea about your objectives. Know what *you* are supposed to do, and do it well. Look straight ahead and keep going— and pray a lot!

I have a little sign on my desk that says, "Attempt something so big that if God isn't in it, it is bound to fail."

That kind of thinking keeps us on track. A friend once told me, "It's not a ministry, unless the Holy Spirit is necessary to make it work."

If we're going to do anything big enough to be truly worthwhile, we'll need the Holy Spirit.

Psalm 37:5 says, "Commit your way unto the Lord . . . and He will bring it to pass."

9

Priorities

PASS THE BATON TO THE CHILDREN

Life is no brief candle to me. It's some burning torch which I've gotten hold of and which I must keep burning high. Someday I must pass it on to coming generations. Our priority has to be the evangelization of our children. God help me—help all of us—not to drop the baton!

In a race, the one who carries the baton and hands it to someone else takes a big risk. Dr. James Dobson talks about this in one of his films on the family. If we don't hand over the baton to our children—the values God gave us and the principles of faith we live by—it doesn't matter how fast they can run.

In our homes and in our work, we must live by the values God communicates to us and pass on those values to those we love.

HE WHO AIMS AT NOTHING
USUALLY HITS IT

Some people spend more time planning their vacations than they spend planning their lives. A friend of mine said that in a book on management, and I think she's right.

I believe every family should have a purpose and a plan for the future, and each member of the family should know what that is.

I remember when I was young and rearing a couple of kids in the city of Dallas and working three jobs. There were many tough times, and I wondered if my kids paid any attention to what I told them or what I did, or if they understood anything about our purposes. But as I mentioned earlier, a recent letter from my grown son showed me that he really had understood.

I believe that if we have a plan and stick to it—having God as our first priority—our children will some day show us what a difference it made. But we may have to wait years to know that. In the meantime, having a purpose and a plan for our lives from the earliest years will give meaning to our daily struggle and help each of us find identity, for commitment to a purpose provides identity.

A TIME FOR EVERYTHING
IN ITS SEASON

Time. Is there ever enough of it to do all we need to do?

Yes, if we recognize that we don't do everything in our lives at the same time.

There is a timing in life—a time to have our children around us . . . a time to nurture and shelter those little ones.

Then there is a time to let them go.

There may be a time to be at home all day. But then there may come the time to be out in the workaday world, if we so desire.

I used to wonder at all the abilities of the talented woman of Proverbs 31. She seemed able to do everything well—a true superwoman. Then my friend Edith Scheaffer pointed out something very important. Those talents were the diversity of a lifetime. She didn't do all those things at once.

Time. There really is enough of it . . . if we let our lives follow their proper timing.

TRUST GOD AND TITHE

One night I was pacing the floor, telling the Lord why I couldn't tithe. I had two children. It was war time. Things were tough.

But as it says somewhere in Proverbs, our reasons sound good—but is the Lord convinced? It was as if He said to me, "Well, Mary, you are not doing such a hot job yourself. Why don't you give Me a chance?"

These verses kept coming back to me: ". . . prove me [trust, me] now herewith, saith the Lord . . . I will . . . open you the windows of heaven, and pour you out a blessing, that there shall not be room enough to receive it" (Malachi 3:10, KJV).

I said, "Okay, God, it is all Your show." I checked "tithe" on my pledge card, and I went to bed. I knew God was going to be up all night anyway, and He would figure it out.

I happened to be working for an insurance company, and about two weeks later a hurricane came and wiped a little town named Goosecreek right off the map. I had to work overtime on Saturdays and nights because of it, so I had extra overtime money which I'd never had before.

At that time a wonderful maid who worked for me and helped with the children said—and to this day she believes it—that God sent that hurricane so I could tithe. No, I say, God didn't send that hurricane so I could tithe, but He used the circumstances for my benefit because I trusted Him.

TITHING . . . NO MATTER WHAT

I've never stopped tithing. Many's the time we would eat cereals for the last two weeks before payday. (I got paid once a month.) The kids would gripe, especially Don. Oh, he would gripe! Yet, you know, about seven years ago when we were building the Mary C. building of First Baptist Church, Dallas, he stood up in church one morning at a special ceremony and he told the congregation, "We used to live out there on Summit Street. We didn't have much money. Many's the time I thought, 'Boy, we sure could use this tithe money.' But this woman was so stubborn and so hard-headed that she said we were going to tithe, no matter what!"

Don added, "But you know, I have seen God pick up that tithe and use it and multiply it beyond our wildest imagination."

I'm like Don. I don't understand the workings of God at all. When it comes to tithing, I don't understand God's mathematics—but I like what He does!

HANDLE MONEY
WITH WISDOM AND GRACE

My grandmother taught me not to buy anything on credit that I wouldn't still have when I got it paid for. That cuts out a lot of things . . . it surely does.

The other day I heard a conversation about borrowing money for vacations and how much interest would have to be paid to borrow the money. Vacations? I just shook my head. How foolish it seemed. What do you have left when you get home? Just the bill. That's all. And you're paying interest on top of that! The misuse of credit in America is one of the things that has gotten us in such a mess. Governments, cities, families—we all need to think about priorities.

Don't borrow money on anything you won't have left after it's paid for. A home. A car. New big things like that are okay. But let's not be foolish. God honors preparation, prayer, and persistence. Let's make prayer our first resource, not our last resort.

I've served on boards of organizations and businesses, and I've heard people make their plans and then piously bow their heads to ask God to bless those plans. I think we should pray first and then plan. God has better plans than we would think of on our own. Why not try God's priorities?

10

Success

WHAT IS YOUR MEASURE OF SUCCESS?

When my children were little, I took in sewing so I could be at home while I worked. That was in the days when you used dress forms to make clothing so a garment would fit each person individually.

A lady would come and I would take her measurements and then I'd adjust the dress form exactly to her shape. The form looked something like a robot, standing in my home. I could sew the dress with that form as a guide, and the dress would always fit. Because I knew the specifications, I could take the dress in at the waist, let it out at the shoulders, get the hem just right all the way around.

Then another lady would come, and I would adjust the dress form exactly to her unique shape all over again. No two of my customers were ever alike. I never tried to use the dress form without adjusting it for every person.

I see many people today who are trying to fashion a formula for success from somebody else's pattern, without any idea that they need to adjust their idea of success to their own needs and personality. I see people blindly following someone else's pattern for life, instead of making their own which fits only themselves. I see them trying to squeeze into someone else's definition, and I know they will be uncomfortable. Too often we try to fashion our lives after the people we see on TV or in other fields of entertainment and sports. Yet each person is unique, with individual gifts—and even with fingerprints like no one else in the world!

What is your measure of success? Only you can design it. You must think carefully, for designing your unique pattern is a demanding task. Fit your definition of success to your own God-given specifications and to the time in your life. Success is a moving target. What is success when we are twenty will be different when we are forty or sixty. When you are planning your life, just remember to ask yourself these questions:

> Is it good for the family?
> Does it bring joy to others?
> Do you feel good about *yourself* in your success
> pattern?

Make your definition of success fit only your own God-given gifts and specifications. You are one of a kind!

BE POSITIVE AND CREATIVE

A high school student was sitting around home for the summer holidays and he decided he absolutely must have a job. He said to his father, "Dad, I've got to go to work."

His dad said, "Well, it's too late to get a job now. You should have started sooner. I don't know where you think you're going to get a job. But let me make a few calls and see if I can help you."

The son said, "No, Dad, I want to get a job on my own." He was quite determined.

So he took the newspaper and began to check the want ads, until he found one that said a company would be taking applications on Monday morning. He planned to arrive early, but when he got there, twenty young men were ahead of him in line. After a few minutes, he decided he had to think of something that would give him an edge, so he pulled a piece of paper from his pocket and wrote on it. Then he took it up to the front of the line and handed it to the secretary of the man who was doing the interviewing.

He said, "It's very urgent that you give this to your boss at once."

The secretary must have thought, *My, if it's that urgent, I'd better take it,* for she carried the note right in to her boss's office. When she gave it to him, he read it and began to laugh.

The paper said, "I am the twenty-first boy in line out here. Don't do a thing until you get to me!"

The young man used his creative genius to get the job. The world is just waiting for people who will use their creative genius.

MONEY—NOT POWER BUT SERVICE

When women work for Home Interiors, if they are quite successful, they find their salaries edging up toward their husband's. And often I tell them we must be careful how we handle money. We have to understand three things about it.

First, money is not power. (Oh, we think it is power. But ideas are power, not money.)

Second, money is not achievement. A woman may start making more money than her husband, or more money than someone else. And she may begin to think that she is a high achiever and that other people who never make a lot of money—pastors, teachers, servants of all kinds—are low achievers. But how wrong she is! These people are great achievers. Money is not achievement.

Third, money is something to be used to bless others. When we understand money that way, life becomes exciting and different. Yes, it is wonderful to have enough money to raise one's family and be comfortable, but money is not given to us to accumulate; it is given to us to *use*. The ability to make money is not a reward for our personal enjoyment. Our abilities and the money we earn are given to us to administer.

Money is not power. Money is not achievement. Money is a means to bless others.

Success is not just a reward to be enjoyed; it is a trust to be administered.

DEVELOP A SERVING HEART

Do you know what the world wants? The world wants service. Develop a serving heart.

You can buy merchandise. You can buy goods. You can buy accessories. But you cannot buy personal caring.

Giving service is our focus at Home Interiors. I know that—no matter what field you are in—*service* will give you the distinctive edge. Both ministry and business require that you serve.

I stayed at a big, well-known hotel during a conference recently. I'm sure the management spent a lot of money advertising this lovely hotel. But when I picked up the phone to call room service, the housekeeping department, or the front office, the first thing a voice said was, "I'm putting you on hold."

That's the same thing as saying, "I'm putting you on *ignore.*"

I needed to get the housekeeping people. The clerk put me on "music," and fifteen minutes passed. I waited, and was doing some other things, and finally I laid the phone down.

I don't call that service! It's amazing how a big company can spend money advertising and then let it all be blown away by a reception clerk who answers the phone and is not service-minded.

Develop a serving heart. Our Lord said, "He who would be great among you must be servant of all."

Our slogan in Home Interiors is, "How can I better serve you?"

Service—that is what the world wants. Service is in such

short supply. The world doesn't need our merchandise. It needs our service.

Are you willing to serve? Do whatever it takes to serve people. If you do, you will be successful.

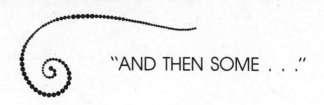

"AND THEN SOME . . ."

Go all out. Don't be a hold-out. Don't be a half-minder.

Did you ever hear people say, "Why, I have half a mind to do such and such"?

Half a mind? You'll never do anything with half a mind!

Put all of your mind, your energy, your strength, yourself into your life work. "And then some."

If your purpose is worthwhile enough, and your belief in it is strong enough, the strength of the purpose will take over and keep you keeping on even when you are physically exhausted.

Do your best—and then some!

IT'S NEVER TOO LATE
TO BEGIN!

It's never too late to begin. A friend of mine was sixty-five years old and had just received his first social security check. He opened it, looked at it, and thought, "Is this really all there is left for me? I'm retired. I'm sixty-five. And I've nothing to look forward to except waiting for the checks to come."

He began to think. As his mind played across the experiences he might draw on to change his circumstances, he remembered his childhood. His parents had both worked and—out of necessity—had taught him how to cook. He'd been a pretty good cook and had even started a restaurant business once, though it had failed. He began casting about in his creative mind to think how to use that experience. . . .

His mother used to make the best fried chicken anywhere, so he searched for her recipe for herbs to coat the chicken. When he found it, he climbed into his old car and started out on the road, thinking he would sell her recipe to someone who wanted to start a business with him. At first he received a lot of "No's." But he kept on until finally someone said "Yes."

At sixty-five, Harlan Sanders was retired on a social security check. At eighty, he was a multi-millionaire, known around the world as Colonel Sanders—originator of Kentucky Fried Chicken. He used his creative genius to discover that it is never too late to begin!

TEACH ME TO SING

You can love me, but I must make me happy.
You can promote me, but I must succeed.
You can teach me, but I must provide the
   understanding.
You can coach me, but I must win the game.
You can lead me, but I must walk the path.
You can pity me, but I must bear my sorrow.

For the gift of love is not a food that feeds me.
It is the sunlight that nourishes what I must finally
   harvest for myself.
If you love me, don't just sing me your song.
Teach me to sing.
For when I am alone, it is then that I will need
   the melody.

(The above was read by Mort Utley at a Sales Management Seminar years ago, and I pass it on to you.)

THE CIRCLE OF SUCCESS

Life is like a circle. You attempt something, and you fail a little. You may even fail a little more. Then you succeed a little.

If you keep on—and if you don't give up—you will succeed even a little more. Then, when you gain a little confidence, you can tackle something bigger. Your first success leads you to feel challenged to take on something new. Then the circle of success and failure begins again.

As long as we're succeeding more than we're failing, we gain confidence. We can never be a success on our own, though. Real success requires a creative power outside ourselves.

Of course, we can't succeed merely by saying, "I'm a Christian, and God is certainly going to take care of me." In the Bible, God honors people who show preparation, prayer, and persistence. God honors hard work.

Preparation. Prayer. Persistence. As long as we remember how surely our God honors work that is honorable, purpose that is true to His principles, and a heart that never gives up, our circle of success will continue as growth in our lives.

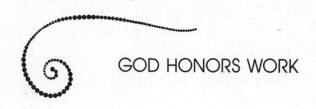

GOD HONORS WORK

My grandmother taught me a verse which reminds me that God is a God of work. It's the second half of that familiar prayer,

> Now I lay me down to sleep,
> I pray the Lord my soul to keep;
> If I should die before I wake,
> I pray the Lord my soul to take.

Grandmother taught me this:

> Now I wake me up to work.
> I pray the Lord I will not shirk.
> If I should die before tonight,
> I pray the Lord my work's all right.

I'm so grateful that I learned this prayer. Grandmother encouraged me to fall in love with work—with the enjoyment of it, the accomplishment of it, the achievement of it. I recommend that you find something to do that you love so much, you will do it for free. Then learn to be so good at it that the world will *pay* you well to do it.

At Home Interiors we have this verse: "If you work for the thing you believe in, you're rich though the way is rough.

"If you're working only for money, you can never earn quite enough."

Fall in love with work. Enjoy it, because God honors it!

11

Everybody Is Somebody

GOD DOESN'T TAKE TIME TO MAKE A NOBODY

I often wear a beautiful diamond watch given me by my friend Ethel Waters. It serves as two reminders: (1) that it was my privilege to be a part of her later years, and (2) that there is no such thing as an unwanted child in God's eyes.

Ethel Waters was born to a fifteen-year-old girl. Her mother was the victim of rape in the slums of Philadelphia. By the standards of today's world, she might have been aborted. But by God's grace she was born and grew to become a model for her people and for all people. She was a star of stage and screen, known for that wonderful song, "His eye is on the sparrow, and I know He watches me."

She gave me the watch shortly before she died. I remember her telling me, "Where I'm going, I won't be needing any clocks."

I attended her funeral at Forest Lawn cemetery in California. There were wires and messages of condolence, love, and respect from around the world. With each message I realized again, there is no such thing as an unwanted child. God doesn't take time to make a nobody.

Everybody is somebody. God has a plan and everybody is precious. Every human being is created in His image, His likeness, His mind. As someone once said, "Though conceived in earthly fashion, we are born of the divine."

God is gracious, and I am somebody.

YOU CAN BE CONFIDENT

I took a poll one time of women across America, and I asked them to write down their three greatest needs—in business, in family, and in society. The number one need was self-confidence.

We can develop faith in God, in others, and in ourselves if we realize what kind of God we serve. He is all knowledge and He is all wisdom. He is all beauty, all-knowing, and He says in His Word that He is who is says He is. "I am that I am." Because He is absolutely trustworthy we can say, in the words of Scripture, "I can do all things through Christ who strengthens me."

Because we know *this God* who keeps His promises, we can have faith in other people. We must believe that other people are special and that they have the potential for greatness. We have to believe that our marketplace and our world is filled with people who respond to genuine service, genuine caring, genuine love. We must believe that other people are God's creation, just as we are.

Finally, we can have faith in ourselves. We must believe that we can do great things because we are God's creation. We must believe that we were created for greatness by a loving God who never leaves our side.

If we believe in a loving God, the creative potential of other people, and the loving intentions of God toward ourselves, we have no choice but to be confident. God is surely with us.

THREE THINGS WOMEN NEED

Women need three things—recognition, reassurance, and security. It's all very simple.

Men, your women need to be told every day, "I love you." If you travel a lot, don't forget to reassure them of that love.

I don't care what the "women's lib" folks say. In the heart of every woman is the nesting instinct put there by our Creator. We want a home and we want to feel safe in it.

When someone asks me how to help the women of America, I say, "Get them off the side issues and come back to recognition, reassurance, and security." Reassure them that what they are doing as women is helping somebody. We weren't made to compete, but to offer our contribution. Women want to believe that they are doing something worthwhile.

Women come into Home Interiors sometimes feeling that they don't have any special abilities. "Oh, I can't make flower arrangements," they say. "I can't stand in front of a group and speak, and I can't hang pictures on the wall very well."

I answer, "I've never seen an application yet that asks you to fill out what you *can't* do. What *can* you do? Find your strengths and build on them. When you come to work with us at Home Interiors, you already can do many things well. Think what they are.

"You are already somebody. So *be* somebody."

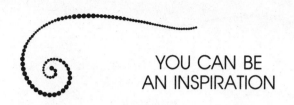

YOU CAN BE
AN INSPIRATION

I sat across from a very distinguished looking gentleman at a dinner not long ago, and he suddenly looked across the table at me and said, "Inspire me."

That's the truth—that's literally what he said.

I shouldn't have been surprised at his words. I believe God created women to be the inspiration of mankind. I often say, "If we don't inspire our men, the poor dears might not get inspired. It's up to us."

I heard a wonderful statesman from Israel say once that no society or culture rises any higher than the standards of its women. I believe that, and I've been ashamed in America by the standards women have let down. We must hold high standards.

And we must be sensitive—to the needs of other people, their feelings, their hurts. Women are known for their sensitivity, and we must turn that sensitivity toward others. Otherwise, we'll turn it toward ourselves and be the type of person who always gets her feelings hurt unless someone constantly recognizes her.

God intended us to turn that sensitivity toward others—to be the antennas of other people's needs. We have what it takes to be the inspiration of mankind. Let's discover that gift, and use it.

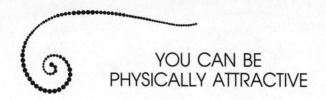

YOU CAN BE
PHYSICALLY ATTRACTIVE

Ruth Graham once asked a group of men what they were looking for in a wife. They said they were looking for "atmosphere" and "scenery." Most of the older ones were looking for atmosphere. Most of the younger ones were looking for scenery.

I think God created women to be especially attractive and beautiful. I remember the words of a wonderful and wise lady who trains our gals at Home Interiors. A long time ago she told them, "From your neck up you show the world what you think of the world. From your neck down you show the world what you think of yourself!"

I think she was right. We need to be as physically attractive as we can possibly be. The Home Interiors standard for women is—

> Be physically attractive
> Be emotionally stable
> Be financially intelligent
> Be intellectually awake
> Be spiritually dynamic.

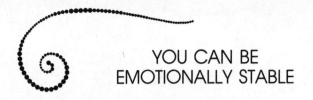

YOU CAN BE EMOTIONALLY STABLE

Be emotionally stable! That's a tall order for women. Our emotions are a little closer to the surface in everything we do. So we have to learn and practice stability, and we have to pray a whole lot. God can help us become the emotionally stable person He has in mind for us to be. I know He can.

I think of Gladys Hunt's book *MS Means Myself.* She said there are many restless women who need to go and sit on God's lap for a while. Corrie Ten Boom once said, "Nestle, don't wrestle with God." Just nestle and rest in His everlasting arms.

Some of you may not have had a normal earthly family. Some of you may have had parents who hurt you deeply. But remember, our heavenly Father does not change. He is always the same. He is kind. He is good. He is loving. He is firm. He hurts when we hurt. He never ceases to love us.

With that kind of love as our base, we can count on God to make us emotionally stable.

YOU CAN BE
INTELLECTUALLY AWAKE

It's not easy to be intellectually awake when you're at home all day taking care of children. Your conversation can drop to a three- or four-year-old level. I think of the wife who had not been out much lately until her husband's company had a big dinner. She found herself seated opposite a company official and she tried desperately to think of something to say. Finally she looked at him and said, "Bet I can eat my spinach before you do!"

Of course, she learned something that night that she and those of us who hear her story will never forget. It takes real work to stay intellectually awake when you are surrounded by so many everyday duties. But we absolutely have to make the effort.

After all, God created us in His image, with what I call a "creative genius mind." I believe God meant us to be the crowning achievement of creation.

He told Adam and Eve to manage the world, to use their genius to build the world, to figure out how to build shelters, make fires, tame the elements and the animals, and even, one day, to fly!

It's exciting to know that we have such potential. We can solve problems, we can soar to the heights, we can communicate with the world. We can do whatever we set our minds to do. Every day is filled with possibility. We are called of God to be intellectually awake.

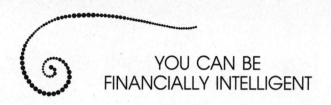

YOU CAN BE
FINANCIALLY INTELLIGENT

I was listening to some young women talk about their financial struggles recently. Their husbands were taking classes in seminary, so they were making some real sacrifices. These women had worked hard to make their homes "cozy," and to adjust to new surroundings and a different atmosphere.

Cozy . . . I knew what they meant by the word *cozy*. They used that word, rather than complain about their cramped living space and their very real financial crunch. It is everlastingly to their credit that they did not use our conversation as a chance to complain. Their attitude was, "These things go with the decision we have made."

I went to speak with them because I was interested in their way of coping. I think women are absolute geniuses when it comes to coping and being resourceful.

I'll always remember the story of the widow woman in the Old Testament who went to the prophet Elijah. Her husband had died and her two sons were about to be sold into slavery to pay off his debts. (That was the custom in those days. I can't help but think how many families would lose their kids if that were the custom now!)

This woman went to the man of God and asked for help. He said, "What do you have in your house?" And she answered, "Not much. A little oil. A little meal."

He said, "Have the two boys go out and gather all the bottles and vessels they can find. Fill them with oil. Sell these vessels until you are out of debt."

And you know, as long as they had the faith to borrow the bottles, the flow of oil did not cease. But when the last available bottle was filled, the oil ceased. They had gained just enough to pay their debts.

That story reminds me of the things in our homes that can be turned into resources to bring in extra money. I used to bake bread and sell it. I made cookies and sold them. Today people make and sell unusual handcrafts. Every woman has lots of skills she can turn into extra resources.

God has put all those resources right at our fingertips, waiting for us. And He is ready to help us become a creative genius for Him.

Let's learn how to be financially intelligent. We have what it takes!

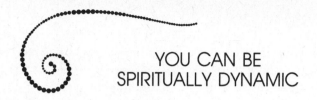

YOU CAN BE
SPIRITUALLY DYNAMIC

Years ago an old missionary told me:

You ask me what is the will of God,
And I will answer true,
It's the nearest thing that should be done,
That God can do through you.

I can't repeat these words often enough. They are the key to being spiritually dynamic. The will of God is "the nearest thing that God can do through you."

Oh, we are such idealists, especially when we're young. We want to save the world, and we are going to go to Africa or Cambodia or India to do it.

Right next door our neighbors need loving and touching and caring in a close, personal way. That's the nearest thing we can do that is truly the will of God. That is where we are privileged to begin.

The nearest thing—sometimes it is baking a loaf of bread and taking it to someone who needs a lift. Sometimes it's reaching out in a special way. Sometimes it's being a faithful prayer partner and helping to build a network of prayer.

Our spiritual strength as women often comes from those networks of prayer. Thousands of women all across this nation hold things together through their prayers. We give each other—and everyone else—the same strength and support women have always provided.

I heard a man say once that men hadn't changed much over the years. Women haven't changed much either. A few generations ago when our ancestors were crossing the prairies or making their way on frontier ranches, or whatever they were doing, grandfather never came in from a hard day and said, "My, you are such an adorable wife. You work so hard. Why don't you get away from that hot stove for a while, and let me take over!"

Women had to find their own sources of inner strength, just as they do today. And they formed support networks, just as we do today, to sustain one another. They had quilting bees and canning sprees. Today women find other ways and reasons for getting together. And as they make prayer a part of their gathering, they contribute to the will of God and to His work in this world.

SUPPORT ONE ANOTHER

Build your own support team. My daughter found she could do this "from scratch" in a brand new community. She and her husband moved to New Jersey after he finished up at Texas A & M University. He went to work with Bell Telephone Laboratories. Right away, my daughter began to go calling on the neighbors.

They thought this rather odd, and said to one another, "That woman from Texas will come visit you. You'd better watch out."

On she went, visiting people and inviting them for coffee and to get acquainted. She found that so many were far from their homes, and feeling very lonely. Soon she had built a little network of wives who could support one another.

She and her family went to visit a Baptist church, but they found it much less friendly than First Baptist Church, Dallas, where everyone is always so warm and outgoing. Nobody spoke. Nobody said a word. My daughter wondered if she'd gone to the wrong place by mistake!

She missed the warmth of God's love. But she realized through that experience that many people go to a church for the first time seeking love. And if they do not find love in the one place they've learned to expect it, then they must wonder what is real in Christianity.

It was a hard lesson, but a good one. She realized how crucial it is that we build loving networks—at home, in the neighborhood, in our churches. We must work together to build loving networks and to hold one another up—in the name of God's love.

12

Love That Work!

PUT OUT
YOUR BEST EFFORT

We don't have to iron much anymore since we have all the wonderful polyester things. But I used to iron a lot. First I would dampen the wrinkled clothes with a little sprinkling bottle and roll them up. Then I would keep them in the refrigerator so they wouldn't dry out. Everyone did that. I'd watch the refrigerator fill up with unironed clothes until I couldn't put off ironing any longer.

I didn't like to iron. But I learned that putting it off was the worst thing I could do. So I started ironing in the first part of the day. Then I could look forward to the rest of the day instead of dreading the time when I'd have to begin!

If I did the things I didn't like early in the morning, I could live with anticipation—live life on tiptoe—all the rest of the day.

Finally I decided that I must do even more—I must learn to find joy in my ironing. I would iron a shirt or a little dress just as beautifully as I could, and then I would hang it up where I could see it. I promised myself that I would sit down with a cup of tea or something after I had done several, and I would just gaze at them and enjoy them.

You know, it became a pleasure to look at all the ruffles so carefully ironed out. I learned to feel very good about my accomplishment—about all those hours spent working at something so carefully. I've decided that if I could learn to enjoy ironing, then anybody can learn to enjoy anything!

FIND JOY
IN YOUR WORK

I like to say that housework is "daily." It's so daily no-body notices it—until you stop doing it.

I like the story about the husband who came home every day and said to his wife, "Well, what did you do all day?"

She always had trouble answering that question because he seemed so unimpressed with her answer.

One night when he came home the beds weren't made, the kitchen table was filled with breakfast dishes, and the entire house had a look of confusion.

"What happened?" he asked in astonishment.

She said, "Well, you know how you always ask me, 'What did you do today?'"

"Yes," he said. "What *did* you do today?"

"That's just it," she said. "Today I *didn't.*"

I've always told that story because it reminds me that we have to brag on ourselves when it comes to housework. It's the kind of thing no one will notice until we stop. And I think we have to find our own kind of joy in it too—whether it's ironing, baking a loaf of bread, or some-thing else. If it's work we've done, we may take joy and pride in it. Remember success is like housework—it is so daily. You have to do it all over again every morning.

FIND PURPOSE
IN DAILY ROUTINE

In our business at Home Interiors we have to pack and unpack a lot of merchandise. Sometimes people say, "Don't you get awfully tired of packing and unpacking?"

"I would," I say, "if I thought of it as packing and unpacking. But I think of it as Christmas. Every time I unpack, I'm anxious to see what is inside the paper. That extra anticipation makes the time go faster and adds a little joy."

If we're going to be happy, we have to put joy in everything we do. Life just kind of goes on. I can tell you that. It is just "daily" for a long long time.

But if you have a purpose—and most of you do, even if you lose sight of it now and then—I promise you that when your physical strength wears out, the strength of the purpose will take over and keep you going.

That purpose must be strong enough and right enough because it is God's purpose for your life. But if it is, it will bring you joy and strength when you need it. I promise you, having a sense of purpose will serve you—it will keep you going when you're tired and will give you a second wind!

LOVE HARD WORK

My grandmother believed in work. She taught me laziness was a sin with a capital "S." She taught us early to work hard, and I learned by helping her cook for her threshing crew. The threshing crew would come in after laboring for hours in the fields. They'd stay until they threshed all the wheat on the farm. Then they'd move on to another one.

You'd think that cooking for a threshing crew would be anything but joyful. But my grandmother made it exciting.

I learned early from her to love to cook and I still love it. I married a man who loves to eat, and I have three grandsons in college and two inherited nephews who love to eat—so it's a good thing I had those early lessons. I learned to take pleasure in working hard in the kitchen. I'm so glad I paid attention to those early lessons.

I'm speaking from experience with this advice: Work hard. Find purpose for every routine in whatever kind of work you have to do. Later on you'll see the wisdom of it!

ADD ROYALTY
TO THE ROUTINE

Marriage and family life need polishing, just like the silver. Keep polishing, add some candlelight, add some royalty to the routine. That's the remedy for the "daily-ness" of life.

When you're first married, everything seems so fantastic for a while . . . the husband even puts on an apron and helps in the kitchen. But pretty soon he doesn't do that anymore, and you need to find some ways to keep the magic in your life—especially toward the end of the month when the money gets scarce.

It's amazing how festive a meal can look when it's served by candlelight. The food looks better. And so do you. At Home Interiors we sell candles because we know what they can do to add that extra touch. Eating becomes "dining" by candlelight.

My husband worked for the government for many years and he always said you could tell when it was close to the end of the month. At lunchtime people would stay in the lunchroom, and they ate a lot more peanut butter during that last week. I lived through the depression, so I'm not afraid of anything. I believe you can make the most mundane circumstances festive.

When my children were little there was a war going on and money was scarce. To make a special dessert, I'd put sugar cubes soaked in lemon extract on top of a single dip of ice cream, light the sugar cubes with a match, and turn off the lights. This dessert was made from the simplest of ingredients, but the kids loved it. When it burned out, they'd want me to light it again and again. I also used the opportunity to talk to them about the real light of the world—Jesus Christ.

Simple things—they are the key to royalty. Add a flower to the table. Light a candle. Write a little note to put in your husband's lunch. (Don't put it inside the sandwich.)

Find little ways to let your husband know you're glad you are married to him. Find ways to let your children know they are special. Find ways to say that life is wonderful and you are glad to share it with them.

THANK GOD FOR YOUR 'SERVANTS'

My nephews recently moved into an apartment. One of them called the other day. "Guess what?" he said. "We even have a dishwasher."

I thought, *I was forty-four years old before I had a dishwasher. Here is this kid with one. Now everyone has "servants."*

We all have servants—dishwashers, electricity, electric irons. I can remember when we put an iron on a kerosene stove to heat it. You rubbed the iron over the clothes, and when it cooled off, you had to heat it up again.

I remember the church I grew up in, in Missouri and another one in Arkansas. They both had the old gas lanterns hanging up to give us light. Then one day we got electricity, and everyone was so excited.

Today we have air conditioning. I thank the Lord every night for Mr. Carrier, who made air conditioning possible for so many of us. It's such a wonderful servant, and how we take it for granted!

Somebody reminded me, "What you say is true. Our grandmothers didn't have all the appliances and things we have. They had to go to the well and draw the water out of a bucket and carry it back to the house. But they didn't have to sit up all night worrying about making payments on the bucket!"

That's true. We pay for our "servants." But we should never take them for granted. We need a thankful attitude.

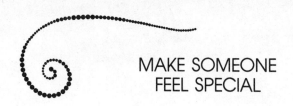

MAKE SOMEONE
FEEL SPECIAL

Every day make someone feel special. Oh, how hungry people's hearts are to feel special.

We would all be surprised how much people who do not look like they need our special touch really need it. Billy Graham reminded me once that everyone needs a special touch, today.

I love those red plates you can buy now that say on the border, "You are special." But you can even make them yourself. Take a paper plate and fix it up with those words on it and add the person's name. Serve a meal, and when the meal is finished, there those words will be, staring up at someone special to you.

We can't do enough to remind people that they are special to us. Use your imagination. The possibilities are unlimited.

13

Fulfillment

FIND FULFILLMENT
IN LIVING

Fulfillment in living depends on just a few things, and the first is: what or whom do you put your trust in?

Every person wants to build a life around something or someone that won't change. But I'll tell you something. Jesus Christ is the only One I know who doesn't change.

How many have put trust in a marriage that didn't work out the way they dreamed? Or in a job that went kaphooey? Some have put their trust in a business and it failed. Others put their trust in intelligence. . . .

I've met Ph.D.s who trust their own intelligence. I met a young woman the other day who said her trust was in the "energy chance theory." She said that was all she needed. But within two weeks a tragedy struck her pretty hard, and she came back and asked for my prayers.

When the chips are down, no theory in the world will hold us up. Our trust in intellect will fail. Our trust in people will fail. Our trust in our own projects will fail. Our trust in self alone will fail.

Paul said in the Bible, "I can do all things through Christ who strengthens me."

If we think we can do for ourselves, the day will come when we fall short. But there is a better way—a way that can never fail. We truly can do all things . . . through Christ.

DELIGHT ONLY IN GOD

We built a chapel near our home, across a little section of creek. On the wall of the chapel we placed some words from the book of Jeremiah that always remind me of life's priorities:

> Thus saith the Lord, Let not the wise man glory in his
>   wisdom,
> Neither let the mighty man glory in his might,
> Let not the rich man glory in his riches:
> But let him that glorieth glory in this,
> That he understandeth and knoweth me,
> That I am the Lord which exercises loving-kindness,
>   judgment, and righteousness, in the earth:
> For in these things I delight, saith the Lord.
>
> Jeremiah 9:23–24, KJV

I placed those words there to remind me that we have only one thing to delight in—that we know God. He is the only thing we can boast about.

I challenge you . . . do you know Him?

WHERE DO YOU FIND
YOUR IDENTITY?

Little Dennis the Menace used to go to the mailbox and pull out the mail, eagerly looking for something. He complained loudly one day—speaking for all of us: "How come all the mail I get says 'Occupant'?"

Nobody wants to be just an "occupant." We want to be *somebody*.

We stop to ask ourselves who we are—in our job, in our home, in the church. We are "somebody" in the real sense of that word when we are part of the body of Christ. Oh, we are so important there. We are accepted. We are redeemed. We are unique.

Unique . . . every thumbprint different. God made us unique. He made us human beings with unlimited potential. We are the special creation of God. Each of us is different, creative, blessed with our own individual genius. We're somebody!

WHERE IS YOUR SECURITY?

"I have to have a job with security." How many times have I heard people say that? And soon they find out that a lot of those "secure" jobs don't have security after all.

"I have to have a job with a set income," they'll say. At Home Interiors, we watch our incomes grow with our potential.

The important question for all of us—no matter what kind of job arrangement we have—is where we find our security.

If we're seeking security in the wrong place, God may shuffle things in our life until we see our mistake. He may shake those foundations until we come to trust only in Him.

And then He'll build so many wonderful things for us— a sure foundation . . . a security that can never fade. But first we have to be looking in the right place for our security. Then everything else will fall into place.

WHERE DO YOU SEEK STIMULATION?

I saw a sorry sight on the front page of the paper the other day: a photograph of Fair Park Stadium, where fifty-seven thousand people had paid eighteen dollars apiece to see and hear The Who. Who? That's a good question. . . . I cut the clipping out and wrote across it, "Some recession!" Eighteen dollars apiece. Fifty-seven thousand people seeking stimulation. . . .

I've always said that we don't have a recession in America as long as our two biggest problems are where to park and how to reduce. But how can we keep from being bored? How can we keep from seeking stimulation in places that can never satisfy?

If we have a relationship with the Lord God Himself, we have an unlimited potential for everything. He will do things through us that we could never even imagine. And we'll have stimulation and a purpose that is right and loyal and true.

If we are willing to work, He will take us to new heights. This is the God who can take just one little boy's lunch and multiply it to feed a multitude. He can do that miracle within each life, as we seek to find our stimulation in Him alone.

14

Launch Out

LET DOWN YOUR NETS AGAIN

One day as Jesus was speaking at the lakeshore, great crowds of people gathered around Him, anxious to hear the word of God. When the crowd became too large, Jesus asked to borrow Simon Peter's boat so that His disciples could row Him out a little way into the lake where he could speak to the crowd and be heard by all.

When He had finished speaking to the crowd, He turned to Simon Peter and said, *"Launch out into the deep, and let down your nets."*

I always feel good about Simon Peter because I can identify with his answer to Jesus. He said, "Master, we have toiled all night long and we did not catch a thing—not one thing. Nevertheless, at your word, I will cast out the nets. I will launch out."

Now Peter was an experienced fisherman. He knew that lake and he had tried everything he knew. When I think about that, I realize how much we are like Peter. It reminds me of a time when I was helping a young woman improve her sales record with our business. When I made a suggestion she would say, "Well, I have done that." She had already "done it" and "it" didn't work—just like Peter.

But Peter had launched out anyway—out into the deep where he had not been before. Or at least, if he had been out in the deep waters, he needed to try one more time.

Do you know . . . his catch of fish was so great that it nearly broke the nets? In fact it did break some of them, and Simon Peter and his crew had to call for other fishermen to help them. The Bible says they were "astonished"—absolutely astonished—at the catch.

DON'T STAY TOO CLOSE
TO WHERE YOU GOT IN

A little boy went to visit his grandparents. Late at night they heard a terrible crash upstairs so they ran to the bedroom and discovered their grandson had fallen out of bed.

He was embarrassed about it, but they had to ask him what happened so they could prevent it from happening again.

He looked at them with his round, sleepy eyes and he said, "Well, I guess I stayed too close to where I got in."

Too close to where he got in! We do that too. We think it's much safer to stay close to the fence. The truth is, that's a sure way to fail. We need to keep on moving forward. Every day, it's time to launch out!

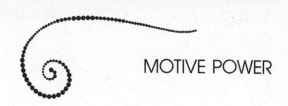

MOTIVE POWER

Do you know where you are? Do you know where you want to go? You must have the answers to those questions, or you'll enthusiastically jump on your great white steed, and go flying off in the wrong direction.

Have goals that are worthy and attainable. Have goals that will make you reach, stretch, and go a little higher than you ever dreamed possible.

Have such great motives that you will truly have "motive power."

I saw motive power in action one day. It happened at a game between the Dallas Cowboys and the Philadelphia Eagles. The Eagles beat Dallas because they came to win! The Eagles played hard and they cheered and applauded each other for every good move. They played as if the game were their Super Bowl. That made all the difference.

Later the Eagles were royally defeated by the Raiders, because they let their motive power diminish. They let another team defeat them without even putting up a fight.

If there is one great talent God gave me, it's that I never give up. I believe you have to "keep on keeping on." You can't just have enough motive power for one time. If you are going to launch out, you don't want to find yourself in deep water and running out of fuel. Let's hold on to continuous motive power!

LIFE HAS NO SHORTCUTS

I have never found a shortcut to success. There is no royal road to learning. I see a lot of people coming into business who think they are going to have this, and do that, and it will all be simple and fast.

I always tell them, "I am pretty smart, and if there had been an easier way, I would have found it. I have been at this a long time."

We must learn to handle rejection. Not everyone is going to accept our plan. Not everyone will want us to display our merchandise in their homes. Not everyone is going to like us, or be interested in what we are interested in.

I like to tell my displayers, "Honey, if every prospective hostess said yes, we would not need you. We would just put a sign up on the warehouse door."

Remember, we will face rejection. How we handle rejection will determine whether or not we have success.

There's just no shortcut. We have to develop motive power, and we have to "stay with it," no matter what.

USE THE IGNITION
OF INSPIRATION

Inspiration is the ignition which lights the fuel in your rocket, propelling your guided missile to "launch out." Inspiration is the willingness to believe that change is possible. It can turn you from an unguided missile into a guided missile, heading in a definite direction toward a worthy goal.

Marva Collins reminds me of the power of inspiration. She is the black teacher in Chicago who quit her job and started teaching children in her home—children the school system said were unteachable. But she soon had them reading Chaucer, quoting Shakespeare, and doing many other valuable things. Her idea grew far beyond the space in her home. Now she has a school of two hundred students, and a waiting list. She had the inspiration to teach children who people said could not be taught.

How did she do it? The children have no recess. The school has no playground. The children work hard. They have only thirty minutes for lunch.

Marva Collins does not have a desk. She is on her feet all day long, going from student to student and leaning over their shoulders to encourage them. She is pushing them to do better than they ever dreamed they could do.

She has given them the ignition they need. Her own internal ignition fires her to believe that it is possible for children to read Shakespeare, it is possible for children to learn, and it is possible for anyone to be turned on to life!

SHAKE OFF THE DUST
OF REJECTION

When Jesus was training His disciples to go out, He told them to pick the houses they would visit—the ones that were "worthy." I looked up the root word for *worthy* and found it means, "meeting a certain standard."

Stay there in that home awhile and minister to them, Jesus said. And if they don't accept you, shake the dust off your feet and go to the next house.

"Don't carry that dust of rejection with you," Jesus was saying. I meet people whose feet are so heavy with rejection dust, they cannot be creative. They act as if "their Mommy" rejected them or someone didn't like them when they were little. But I say, we have all been rejected by someone at some time. Jesus knew it, too, because He knew human nature. So He said, "Shake the dust off your feet."

He didn't want to hear Peter saying to John, "Did you see what that woman did at the last house we visited? I don't know whether we are on the right mission or not."

And Peter might answer, "I wonder if we have hooked up with the right guy. People don't seem to like us. We'd better go back to Nazareth because we sure must be in the wrong business. Either that, or this isn't the right town for us. I wonder if we should move on."

Jesus would say, "Don't let that dust of rejection cling to you. Shake it off. Don't worry about people. I will take care of you."

TURN OFF THAT
REJECTION TAPE

Some of us play a rejection tape over and over in our heads. It gives us an excuse not to go to sales meetings, to church, or any place where we'll be near successful people. For comfort, we'll call up someone else to commiserate, and we'll play that rejection tape to one another, grinding it into our minds a little bit more with each conversation.

"I don't think I'll go to the sales meeting today," we say.

"Looks like we tied up with the wrong outfit," our co-commiserator replies. "I know they all know I'm failing. I don't have any sales to report, and my manager is always waiting for me."

The dust gets thicker and thicker and pretty soon both people are immobilized by the rejection dust. If you go to the sales meeting feeling that way, you'll seek out somebody else in the back row and you'll sit down and start talking negatively and play that rejection tape all over again.

If you're the one who has to listen to that tape, I recommend getting up and moving with a simple, "Excuse me, please, I have to move." The contaigion of rejection is like smoke. You cannot tolerate it. You must separate yourself from it.

Don't let anybody or anything discourage you. Instead, just say or think to yourself, "Poor thing."

Sometimes it is a member of your family, and with a flick of their shoulder or eyebrow they can say, "You are going to do something—sell something . . . ?" And you can feel rejected on the spot if you don't watch out. Of course, that kind of negativism would just turn me on. Man, would I show them!

You see, they don't understand that you *are somebody* and you *can* do your own launching out.

TRY AGAIN AND AGAIN

A little girl was in a park after Christmas, learning to roller skate. An old man sitting on a park bench watched her closely. She would fall down and get up again and fall down once more. (My elbows hurt, just thinking about it.)

Then the little girl took an especially bad fall, and the man called out to her, "Honey, why don't you just give up?"

Shakily, she pulled herself to her feet, looked the man straight in the eye, and said, "Mister, I didn't get these skates to give up with!"

We're like that little girl. All of us have had days that "skinned our elbows." There are times when it feels like "National Cancellation Week," especially when you're in sales. But we must never forget about the apostle Peter who told the Lord he had fished all night and caught nothing. "Lord," he said, "You want me to try again?"

Because he refused to give up, he was astonished at the results. I want you to refuse to give up, too. You will be astonished at what God can do through you!

15

Momentum

HELP FOR THOSE UPHILL CLIMBS

Momentum works for you when you are going up a hill, and works against you if you ever start rolling down. When I was a child in the country, we used to roll an old tire down the road. Once we'd get it going, it would just keep turning and turning and we could run along beside it and tap it to keep it going. But if it hit a chuckhole, down it went, and we had to spend a lot of energy getting it up again. If we took that rolling tire down a hill, it went so fast that it would pull halfway up the next hill through its own momentum.

Life works by the same principles as the tire. Did you ever see anybody *coasting* through life? Beware, because if you are coasting, the subtle direction you are taking is sure to be downhill. Will you have enough momentum to get up again? It takes a lot of effort to be ready for those uphill climbs.

Don't coast. Develop momentum!

GET OUT OF THE RUT

It is easier to fail and to stay a failure than to be a success and get out of the rut. Most people are comfortable in the rut. I used to wonder why that is so, but I've learned that it's because it takes so much effort to get *out*. People who have failed most of their lives find it comfortable to go on that way. For those who fail and fail, as a continuous pattern, there has to be a revival of the "can do" feeling to make them get up and move out.

I've known displayers for Home Interiors who say, "Well, I could win a mink, or I could win a trip, but I really think I should be at home more. Besides, I have back trouble, and my health just won't let me try harder."

I've seen people with lots of trouble and ailments who got into this business, became inspired and excited, and forgot their problems. They got outside of themselves!

Lois Thomsen, our marvelous manager, comes to mind. . . . When she was fifty her doctor said to her, "Lois, get into something exciting and interesting. Your children are grown now, and if you don't do something, you will be like a lot of women who come to my office. You will be sick. You will find a pain here, and another one there. And you'll feel hurt because your children don't call you. Get into something now that will take you outside of yourself."

She took that advice, and her doctor said he could not catch her once a year for a physical!

Get out of your rut. Get outside of yourself. Help someone else who needs you. The harder you work, the better you'll feel. Most of the work in this world has been done by people who did not feel like it at first. But when you get up and go on, when you do something and the excitement starts to build, when you feel motivation growing and you see people respond to you, you'll never want to sit in that rut again!

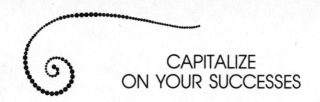

CAPITALIZE
ON YOUR SUCCESSES

A salesman was making a "ho-hum" living selling sausage casings to packing houses. At a sales seminar he heard the leader say, "Your greatest sales power is right after you've had a big week." He went home and thought about that.

Later that night he was awakened by a fire siren and he heard on the radio that one of the biggest packing houses in town was on fire.

He told his wife, "That is one of my customers. I have to go over there and see if there is anything I can do." He arrived and discovered that the fire was in the area where most of the sausage casings were stored. He stayed out all night, helping the purchasing agent inventory the ruin and list what was needed to get back into business. He worked with the agent until noon the next day. He had gone to the business to help, but he was rewarded by the biggest sale of the year.

He was very tired, covered with soot, when he climbed into his car to drive home. As he drove along, he thought how wonderful a shower and his bed would feel. Then the words of the seminar came to him, "Your greatest sales power is just after you have made your biggest sale."

He turned his car around, drove across town to a big packing company to which he had never been able to sell anything, and walked in. The secretary had never let him through before, but there was something about the way he walked up to her desk and said he wanted to speak to the purchasing agent that got her attention. So she let him in.

He said to the agent, "You know, I have never been able to sell you anything . . . never been able to reach you . . .

but I believe my company can service you well. I'd like to have a chance to prove what kind of service we can give."

The agent was impressed with this commitment and with the soot-covered man's story. When the salesman left that place he carried with him his second largest order of the year. Within twenty-four hours he had sold more than during his entire year's work.

He had discovered the secret of momentum.

REMEMBER TO FOLLOW
THROUGH

Commitment means that you will follow through long after the atmosphere in which you made that commitment is gone. It means you'll follow through when you get home and the dishes are in the sink and the kids need attention and hubby needs attention and everybody is pulling at you. It means you'll follow through when something happens and your motivation drains out.

That drained feeling comes to us so easily. It happens when we are high and lifted up in a spiritual sense and then somebody aggravates us to pieces and we blow it!

Coach Tom Landry tells his Dallas Cowboys that commitment is making up your mind and following through—no matter what. Satan loves to give us a little bit of discouragement to cool us down. It's an old tool, and if we can be discouraged just enough to move away from our goal, then the damage is done. A voice seems to say to us, "Who do you think you are? You can't do it."

I have learned that I cannot stop working because someone might not understand, or might criticize me. I have to follow through. I must do my job like a soldier. I have to take that hill, even if the bullets are coming at me.

BE THE CHAIRMAN
OF YOUR BOARD

Draw a little circle on a piece of paper. Put yourself at the top of the circle.

That circle represents your Board of Directors. You are the chairman of your own life's board of directors.

On that board of directors put the names of the people who are actually on your life's board. Who are the people you listen to? Who are the people who counsel you? Who are the people who care enough about you to really have an input into your life? We all have a board of directors at this very minute.

Ask yourself, "How many of those people on my life's board of directors care enough to confront me if I'm wrong, to fire me up when I'm down, to tell me I need to do better?" How many of your board of directors are inspiring and motivating people?

Be sure that the persons you are following—the persons you listen to on your life's board of directors—are going toward a destination you desire. You will follow and listen to people who inspire you, but you are the chairman of the board!

WHEN YOU HURT, GET UP AND GO

Sometimes you will be hurt. Sometimes you will feel like staying home, bawling it out. Sometimes you just want to pull the whole rug in on your hurt. You have been treated unfairly. Things have been extra tough.

That is the time when you have to get up! Get out of yourself. Say, "God, just help me not to feel sorry for myself, but to get up and see what you have waiting for me."

I think of Dr. Francis Schaeffer, who was one of the world's greatest Christian thinkers. He had been so active and so vibrant all his life, writing books, holding seminars, preparing the movie, *Whatever Happened to the Human Race?* Then he developed a malignancy. I can still see him as he was after he became sick—that vibrant man with his little bit of wispy hair and increasing frailty. He was still his dear and alert self. He just never stopped doing what was most important—the things he believed God had given him to do.

Anytime we feel a twinge of self-pity, we need to get up and move out of ourselves. We must find somebody to do something for. We must get up! Get out!

FOLLOW FIVE
SIMPLE GUIDELINES

I have four practical guidelines, and a fifth which says it all. First the four:

- Learn all you can about your business.
- Learn everything you can about people.
- Be absolutely honest.
- Keep your priorities straight.

- And most important of all: Never give up!

I love the story about Winston Churchill, the prime minister of England during World War II. He was invited to give the graduation speech at Eaton, the school where he had gone as a boy.

All the young men of the school sat waiting to hear this great man give them a long speech, full of words of wisdom.

Winston Churchill stood up and looked out at the crowd for a minute.

Then he said, "Never . . . never . . . never give up!"

That's all he said. Then he sat down.

Never give up!

NEVER GIVE UP

The great Russian writer, Solzhenitsyn, tells the bravest story I've ever heard to encourage us not to give up. In the Russian prison where he was, no one was allowed to speak. There was nothing to read, and no encouragement of any kind to sustain life. He said the strain and repression from this atmosphere had set in so badly that he thought, *I will never get out of here.* So he considered taking his own life. He knew that if he tried to escape he would be shot, but he thought, *At least, that will be the end of that!*

His faith would not allow him to do that, though. When day came, he was taken out early in the morning to work and when a break in the work day came, he sat under a tree. He even placed his hand behind him, up against the tree he leaned against, ready to push off and run. Just then a shadow came across the grass and a fellow prisoner sat down beside him. They could speak no words, but he looked into the eyes of the new man who had recently come as a prisoner and saw something he had never seen in any face in prison before—a message of love and concern.

As their eyes locked in silence, they started communicating in their souls and the prisoner took a step forward and drew a cross on the ground with a stick.

Solzhenitsyn said new hope surged within him at that moment. Jesus does love me. He is in command. It is not hopeless!

Three days later he was released from that prison. At his release he learned that many people had been praying for him. He knew with powerful certainty that God is sovereign and there is still hope.

We mustn't give up! We might be the one to communicate hope to someone else, maybe by a gesture, maybe without words. We must love and pray and hold one another up.

16

The Kingdom of Heaven

SEEK YE FIRST . . .

Remember the rich young ruler who came to Jesus by night? He said, "Good Master, what can I do to inherit eternal life?" He was seeking life and liberty and the pursuit of happiness.

Jesus answered by telling him about the Ten Commmandments and their summary in the two great commandments—to love God and neighbor. The young man said, "All these have I kept from my youth up." So Jesus said, "Go and sell all that you have and give it away, and then come back."

The young man went away sorrowing, for he had great possessions. He saw he had not really kept all the commandments. The first one commands, "Thou shalt love the Lord thy God with all thy heart, with all thy soul, and with all thy might." Possessions cannot have first place.

Jesus wasn't trying to make this man wander the earth poverty-ridden. There is no virtue in poverty, especially where health is impaired and people fight among themselves and struggle for the barest existence. Jesus asks us to alleviate those conditions.

But Jesus wanted this rich young ruler to look at his heart—to see where he was placing his values. When I think of that rich young ruler walking sadly away, I want to say, "Come back! Come back! Give it all away, and Jesus will give you more than you can ever imagine of the things that will last. You will be truly happy."

That is what Jesus wanted him to understand. And it's as true today as it ever was: "Seek ye first the kingdom of God—and all these things will be added unto you."

CLING TO GOD'S PROMISES

When God tells us to do something we think is going to be awfully hard, we have to cling to a promise. With that promise, we can follow the commandment.

Think about Abraham, who in his old age became the father of Isaac. Imagine Abraham watching that child grow up, adoring him so much. Then think how Abraham must have felt on that day when God said, "Abraham, I am going to ask something of you. I want you to take your son, your only son, and go up the mountain to sacrifice him."

Abraham must have struggled all night. I can imagine him as he wrestled with that command, thinking, "Oh, but God, You promised that through him would come a great nation!" Early the morning of the next day he arose and took Isaac and a bundle of boards and a torch, and went high up into the mountain to do as God had said.

Because Abraham had settled in his mind to do as God said, he had to cling to a promise. Abraham knew God had promised a whole nation through Isaac. So he went through with all he was told to do. And at the very last minute an angel came to him and stayed his hand from taking the sacrificial stroke.

It was as if God had said, "Abraham, all I wanted to know was if you loved Me more than anything else." God was keeping Abraham from possessing Isaac.

The only way we can possess anything is to give it to Jesus and let go.

We must pray a lot, clinging always to God's promises. He will teach us to "seek first His kingdom," and then we will find God faithfully "adding all these things" unto us.

In Rembrandt's painting as Abraham hears God's voice the knife is literally flung from his hand in victory as if Abraham is saying, "I knew You would come—I knew I could count on You." Yes, we can count on the promises of God.

GET UP AND WALK

Jesus never commanded anybody to do anything He didn't give them the ability to do. I think of the man who had the withered arm. He came to Jesus and Jesus said to him, "Stretch forth your arm."

I can imagine the man thinking, "Jesus, can't you see my arm is withered? It doesn't 'stretch forth.' What do you mean, asking me to do that?"

We do the same kind of thinking today. Jesus gives us a task, and we say, "Me? I can't do that. I can't tell people about Jesus. I get tongue-tied and don't know what to say. I can't go and talk to that person. And I can't go and say I am sorry—will you forgive me? I just can't do what you ask."

When the man standing before Jesus thought to himself, *I can't stretch forth my arm,* He felt Jesus saying to him, "Do it." He gives us the ability to do something, if He tells us to do it.

Remember Jesus saying to the man lying on the pallet, "Son, thy sins are forgiven thee. Get up and walk." After Jesus spoke, the man was able to get up from his bed. Jesus made it possible.

We must remember that Jesus only asks us to do what He enables us to do.

My friend Charles Allen says, "There are three things you can do when you are sick: You can lie on your bed and talk. You can sit on the bed and squawk. Or you can get up from that bed and walk."

When we know our Lord has given us something to do, we must believe that we can do it.

FINDING THE KINGDOM
OF HEAVEN

What does it mean to seek first the kingdom of heaven? Jesus said in the Lord's Prayer, "Our Father, who art in heaven . . . Thy will be done on earth as it is in heaven." We will discover several things about the kingdom of heaven as we go on. Mainly, we will discover that it is the society where God's will is done in earth as it is in heaven.

Only the person who does the will of God will be a citizen of the kingdom. We say, "Lord, I don't even know Your will sometimes. How can I do it? How can I be a citizen of the kingdom when I don't even know *that?*"

We can do God's will only when we realize our own helplessness—when we come to the place where we can say, "I cannot do this by myself." Then we discover that—whatever our task—we are able to put our whole trust in Him. One day a woman was taking her first airplane ride. She was anxious and afraid and the stewardess came by and asked her how she was doing. "Are you comfortable?" she asked.

"Well, I haven't put my whole weight down yet," was her answer!

We are like that with God's everlasting arms, aren't we? We say, "God, I will trust You a little bit, but I can't let my whole weight down yet."

I'm always amazed at people who will trust God with their eternal destiny, but they won't trust Him with their everyday finances. If He can sustain everything around us, He surely can manage the budget. We need to put our whole weight down on Him.

It is hard to live a whole life with half a heart.

We must give God our complete obedience. Obedience is founded on trust. Proverbs 3:15 says, "Trust in the Lord with all your heart, and do not lean on your own understanding" (NASB). Trust comes first, and then obedience. If our children trust us, and if they know that we have their best interests at heart, they will come a lot closer to obeying us. We can trust God because He surely has our interests in His heart. Obedience does not come easily, but it brings us joy.

When we learn to trust and obey, we will be very close to the kingdom of heaven.

17

Beatitude Living

BLESSED ARE
THE POOR IN SPIRIT

In His magnificent Sermon on the Mount, Jesus describes some of our most basic spiritual needs.

First of all, He says, "Blessed are the poor in spirit."

Words have so many different meanings. Most of us think of the word *poor* differently than Jesus meant it. One writer says Jesus meant "the blessedness of possessing nothing." And yet God gave us a world full of beautiful things— mountains and sunsets and a thousand other gifts. He gave us a love of color and beauty.

I know some Christians who think our world should be bare of anything lovely and attractive. I want to tell them, "Look up there at that mountain. Do you think God should just smooth it all out?"

God's concern is with our heart, Jesus says. Our trouble begins when we force God out of His central shrine and allow possessions to take His place. We crowd God out with our collection of moral dust, our stubbornness and aggressiveness, our fighting among ourselves for first place on this earth.

Something in the human heart is greedy and wants to grab. The Master Surgeon trains and loves us and takes away that urge to possess everything and everyone.

The pronouns *my* and *mine* look innocent enough in print, but their constant use is significant. They express the way the roots of our hearts have grown into things, instead of "down deep into His wonderful love" as it says in the Book of Colossians.

We must shift our hearts from a possessive attitude to one of casting every bit of life and trust on Jesus Christ. When we do that, we will know the blessedness of being poor in spirit, for there lies the key to happiness.

BLESSED ARE THOSE
WHO MOURN

Sometimes I have to read again the promise, "Blessed are they that mourn, for they shall be comforted." Problems come so thick and fast that we sometimes have to bow our heads and ask God for comfort in the midst of tragedy. Jesus said we will be blessed as we mourn.

Sorrow is part of life. If we have not experienced it, we will, no doubt, find ourselves among people who have. It helps me to remember this paraphrase of Jesus' words: "Blessed is the person who has endured the bitter sorrow that life can bring." When things go well, it is possible to live for years on the surface of things. But when sorrow comes, a person is driven on to the deep things of life. If he accepts sorrow rightly, a new strength and beauty enter his soul.

The Arabs have a saying, "All sunshine makes a desert." That saying reminds me of this poem:

> I walked a mile with Pleasure.
>   She chattered all the way,
> But left me none the wiser
>   For all she had to say.
>
> I walked a mile with Sorrow,
>   And ne'er a word said she;
> But, oh, the things I learned from her
>   When Sorrow walked with me!
>
> —Robert Browning Hamilton

SORROW IS OUR TEACHER

Sorrow and grief teach us two things. They teach us how many of our friends and associates care. And they teach us how much God cares.

When Jesus' friend Lazarus died, Jesus went to the family. His first obstacle was to get past Martha's limited faith. He said to Martha, "Take me to the tomb." She hesitated, but then she took Him. On the way, He met many mourners. Then we are told that "Jesus wept." I believe He wept because He saw and felt genuine grief.

When my son Don was badly injured in an airplane accident, I stood by his bed and saw his broken body and heard his labored breathing. I felt God saying to me, "I understand. I, too, saw My Son broken, helpless, and wounded. I understand."

I can hardly explain the comfort God brought to me. If you had been there with me, you would have known it too. In my sorrow, I learned that God does care.

BLESSED ARE THOSE WHO MOURN FOR THE WORLD

I talked to Franklin Graham and Ted Dienert after they returned from Cambodia. Franklin told me about a man who died in his arms. He was thirty-four years old, and he appeared to be sixty-five. He had starved to death. The dying man said to him, "Why did you wait so late to come?"

Charles Colson and an elected official experienced this same remorse when they visited a prison in this country. After their visit, Colson's companion came out of that prison and said, "Forgive me. I have asked God to forgive me. I have been in that prison before, but I have never been past the warden's office. I have never been down in those cell blocks where there are two and three men in cells large enough for only one." This man was beginning to understand Colson's concern to separate violent prisoners from the nonviolent. He had heard the prisoners talk of the terror they endure.

They told him of one night when a group of prisoners overpowered the guards, took their guns, broke into the pharmacy to get high on drugs, and then brutally killed other prisoners, including one nineteen-year-old fellow detained the day before and placed in prison for lack of space anywhere else.

When we hear and see these things, we experience sorrow for the sin and guilt and hurt and suffering of the world. We feel we must somehow do our very best to keep as much of this as we can from happening.

In our sorrow, we also remember that Jesus wept over Jerusalem.

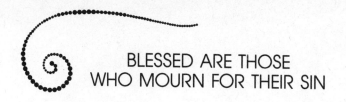

BLESSED ARE THOSE
WHO MOURN FOR THEIR SIN

A person who is sorry for what his sin has done to God and to the world will indeed be comforted. Jesus said, "Whosoever will come unto me, I will in no wise cast out." It's amazing that we just can't be too bad for Jesus to take us when we come to Him.

The blind beggar was sitting by the side of the road calling for help and repentance as Jesus was entering Jerusalem. Amid all the noise and clatter of the crowd he called, "Son of David, have mercy on me." The people told him to hush, but Jesus heard him above all the crowd.

I've often wondered—with all the people in this world calling for God's attention and praying to Him—how can He hear me? But He does—and He can!

Jesus said to the beggar, "What do you want Me to do for you?"

Would we have to stop and think—oh, my goodness, what *do* I want God to do for me? If God gave us three wishes, would we know what they should be? Blind Bartimaeus had no hesitation. "I would like to see again," he said.

"He who seeks will find," Jesus says. "Knock, and the door shall be opened unto you." The way through that door is repentance. There is no other way but through the joy of forgiveness and the sorrow of a broken heart.

What does it mean, "Blessed are those who mourn"? It is the joy, the blessedness, the bliss of the person whose heart is broken for the sin and suffering of the world, and for his own sin. Out of that sorrow, we find the joy and comfort of God.

THANK GOD FOR DIFFICULTIES

Thank God for difficulties as well as blessings. I often say, "Thank Him for the bruises as well as the blessings." Sometimes we learn more from the hurt of our bruises.

But it is hard to give thanks in all things. Not all things seem good. Not all things *are* good. Yet we can give thanks that God is in control, that He loves us, and that He makes things turn out all right.

There is a little saying that I often quote: "God will mend a broken heart, if we give Him all the pieces." Many times we want to keep some of the pieces to ourselves.

Jesus told us, "Lo, I am with you always, even unto the end of the age." I held on to that saying many times as I was raising my family. He promised, "In the world you will have tribulation, but be of good cheer. I have overcome the world!"

When we hang on to the great Overcomer, we don't have to be anxious in the midst of our difficulties. He will bring us through.

BLESSED ARE THE MEEK— WHO HAVE FOUND THE CENTER WAY

To be meek is to live the God-controlled life. Hundreds of years ago, the great philosopher Aristotle said the word *meek* means the "happy medium." Meekness is the right way—the center way—between two extremes.

That means, blessed are those who can get angry at the right things at the right time and not angry at the wrong things at the wrong time. Or, blessed is the person who is neither stingy nor too free-spending, but has learned the right way to be generous.

The meek person can have righteous indignation about things that need to be changed, and yet not carry hurt feelings against others along with that indignation. The meek person refuses to give up the faith because of something someone has done that does not live up to the high standard of Christ.

I tell my grandchildren, "Don't put your faith in a person. Don't put it in the church or in a teacher. People will let you down. Put your faith in Jesus Christ, and He will make it right and never let you down. Never!"

Trust in His perfect meekness, and He will hold you to the center way.

THE MEEK ARE THE
BEST LEARNERS

Blessed are the meek . . . those who have the humility to know their own ignorance and weakness and need. Those with this meekness will inherit the earth, Jesus said. It is a fact of history that the man with the gift of self-control, the man with his instincts, passions and impulses under discipline, is the one who becomes great.

The truly meek are the best learners in the world, for without humility we cannot learn anything. Quintilian, the great Roman teacher of oratory, said that some of his scholars would have been excellent students if they were not already convinced of their own knowledge. No one can teach the person who "knows it all" already.

Without humility there can be no learning, no love, and no religion. For all these things carry with them a sense of our own unworthiness. We only reach true maturity when we are conscious that we are the creature and the learner, while God is the Creator. Without God, we can do nothing *of eternal value.*

BE MEEK . . .
BUT NOT SPINELESS

Moses, the greatest leader and law-giver in the world, was "very meek above all men on the face of the earth," the book of Numbers says. Certainly Moses was no "milk and water" character. He was anything but spineless. He challenged the throne of Pharaoh—at the right time. He learned to have his anger "on a leash."

In Proverbs 16:32 we learn, "He that ruleth his spirit is better than he who taketh a city." Alexander the Great lost everything because he lacked that quality of a "ruled spirit." During a fit of uncontrolled temper in the middle of a drunken orgy he hurled a spear at his best friend and killed him.

No one can lead others until he has mastered himself. The person who has given himself to the complete control of God will gain this meekness which God says enables us to "inherit the earth."

No one—man or woman—can be a manager in any business without first learning to control himself or herself. But the person who has given herself completely into the control of God will gain meekness and humility. The result will be a good manager—one who has the inner capacity and character to "inherit the earth." More than that, once we are truly meek we will be able to help others discover that same inheritance of blessedness which God has granted to us.

BLESSED ARE THOSE
WHO HUNGER AND THIRST
FOR RIGHTEOUSNESS

If you've ever seen a film of the Holy Land, or visited there, you know that it is a long way across the desolate desert from one waterhole to the next—especially when all you have is a little skin filled with water. The people to whom Jesus said, "Blessed are those who thirst for righteousness," knew the agony of thirst.

Eddie Rickenbacker's book, *Other Hands Than Ours*, describes his ordeal in the Pacific after he and his men raided Tokyo. Their plane went down in the ocean, and they were adrift for several days. Surrounded by salt water, they faced the temptation to slake their thirst with water they could not drink. When I read his book, I would go and get myself a glass of water, just reliving with him how terribly thirsty he was. Rickenbacker tells how, after they prayed, the flesh of a seagull was sufficient to satisfy their hunger and thirst.

Oh, the terrible thirst that comes to a person who does not have water! Jesus says that the person who is as desperate for righteousness as a person who longs desperately for water will find the goodness of God. When we truly long for God with all that is within us, He will meet us in our search, and we will be satisfied.

REAL GOODNESS
REQUIRES SACRIFICE

We have to be thirsty enough to truly seek before we will find. How much do we want a right relationship with God? The desire for real goodness requires a sacrifice—giving up our own will.

Jesus never said, "Blessed are those who are good." He said, "Blessed are those who long for goodness." God is sympathetic to the strugglers in life.

"He that is in you is mightier than He that is in the world." Blessedness comes to those who—in spite of failures and failings—still cling to the impassioned love of the Highest.

We need to choose very carefully whom we follow and what we admire, for we will become like whatever we admire and worship.

I think of the story of the great stone face high up on a mountain. A little boy lived in the valley near the side of the mountain and looked up every day at that face, admiring its strongly etched features. When he grew up, people said he looked very much like that stone face—with strength and honor etched into his own features.

The greatest lesson in life is to "seek first the kingdom of God and His righteousness," for after that first priority, all other things will be added unto us, and we will be molded according to our priorities.

Blessing, happiness, joy—these come only to the person who hungers and thirsts for righteousness more than for anything else.

BLESSED ARE THOSE
WHO DREAM OF GOODNESS

Most people have an instinctive desire for goodness. Only a few suffer from what the poet Robert Louis Stevenson once described as the "malady of not wanting." What a big difference it would make in the world if we literally dreamed of and desired goodness more than anything else!

The command to seek goodness and righteousness is a frightening beatitude. But comfort comes in the fact that it includes not only those who *achieve* goodness, but those who *long* for it with all their heart, even if they only partially achieve it.

If blessedness came only to the person who achieved, then few would be blessed. But blessedness comes to the person who—in spite of failures and failings—still clutches to an impassioned love of God.

The writer H. G. Wells said once that a man may be a bad musician and yet be passionately in love with music. Robert Louis Stevenson spoke of those who sink to the lowest depths "clutching the remnants of virtue to them, in the brothel and on the scaffold." Sir Norman Birkett, the famous lawyer and judge, was speaking with criminals once and he mentioned the "inextinguishable something in every person"—the "implacable hunter" which is always at our heels. He reminded those criminals that the worst of men are "condemned to some kind of nobility."

The true wonder of man is not that we are sinners, but that—even in our sin—we are haunted by goodness. Even in the mud, we can never wholly forget the stars!

David always wished to build the temple of God. He never achieved that ambition. It was denied and forbidden to him, but God said to him in 1 Kings 8:18, "Thou didst well that it was in thine heart."

In His mercy, God judges us not only by our achievements, but also by our dreams. If at the end of the day we are still hungering and thirsting for goodness, we are not shut out from His blessedness.

It is in our seeking that Jesus comforts us and comes to us and rewards us with His own presence.

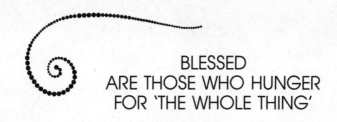

BLESSED ARE THOSE WHO HUNGER FOR 'THE WHOLE THING'

The words *hunger* and *thirst* in the beatitudes are verbs of longing for the "whole thing"—not just some part of God's goodness. The words really mean, "Blessed are those who hunger and thirst for the whole of righteousness, the total and complete portion of righteousness."

That longing for the "whole" is what people seldom exercise. We are content with a part of righteousness. A man might be a good man in the sense that—however hard we tried—we could not pin a moral fault on him. His honesty, his morality, his respectability might be beyond question. But no one could go to that man and weep out a story of failure on his breast. Anyone who tried to do that would be frozen out.

Goodness—partial goodness—can be accompanied with hardness, censoriousness, lack of sympathy.

On the other hand, a person may have all kinds of faults. A person may swear, gamble, lose his temper, and yet give away his last penny and the very coat off his back. That is admirable but that, too, is partial goodness.

In "total goodness," the kind Jesus asks us to seek, neither thoughtless righteousness nor faulty warm-heartedness is enough.

BLESSED
ARE THE MERCIFUL

Most people are so concerned with their own feelings that they are not much concerned with the feelings of anyone else. When they are sorry for someone else, it is from the outside. They do not try to get inside the other person's mind and heart—to see and feel things as she sees and feels them.

To feel as others feel takes a deliberate effort of the mind and will. It requires a conscious identification with the other person—a feeling of being "inside the other person's skin."

Jesus Christ, in the most literal sense possible, got inside the skin of mankind. He came to us as a man, seeing things, feeling things, thinking things just the same as you and I would experience them. God knows what our life is like because God came right inside life.

When Queen Victoria lost her husband, Prince Albert, she was left alone. At that same time, a friend named Mrs. Tulloch lost her husband. When Queen Victoria went to visit Mrs. Tulloch, the friend was resting on a couch and she struggled to rise quickly and to curtsy. Said Queen Victoria, "My dear, don't rise. I am not coming to you today as a queen to a subject, but as one woman who has lost her husband to another." She understood the principle of showing mercy—experiencing another's thoughts from the inside.

When we learn to enter into a person's thoughts and feelings in that way, we shall indeed discover the blessing promised to those who are merciful. The fifth beatitude means:

"Oh, the bliss of the one who gets right inside other people until she can see with their eyes, think with their thoughts, feel with their feelings . . . for she will know that God in Jesus Christ has done exactly that for us."

LET YOUR MERCY
BE APPROPRIATE

In showing mercy, we must be saved from being kind in the wrong way. The story of Mary and Martha at Bethany reveals the right and wrong way to show mercy. Jesus visited these friends at a time when the cross was only a few days ahead. He came to their home to rest and relax, to lay down the terrible tension of living.

Martha loved Jesus. He was her most honored guest. Because she loved Him, she wanted to provide the best meal the house could supply. She bustled and scurried here and there with the clatter of dishes and the clash of pans. All Jesus wanted was quiet.

Martha meant to be kind, and she could hardly have been more thoughtless. But Mary understood that Jesus wished only the peace and quiet. She sat with Him and listened to Him.

So often, when we wish to be kind, kindness has to be given in *our* way, and the other person has to put up with it, whether he likes it or not. Our kindness would be doubly kind—we would be saved from much unintentional lack of kindness—if we would only make the effort to get inside the other person.

In our homes we often bake something for the family, when all they want is for us to sit and listen to them for a while. We give them what *we* want to give them, instead of what they need.

To be truly merciful, we must understand what a person feels and needs. We will be able to forgive because we understand why a person exhibits behavior which troubles us. If someone is irritable or discourteous, he may be worried or in pain. As the French proverb says, "To know all is to forgive all."

When we make the deliberate attempt to get inside the other person's mind and heart, we will be able to give real and appropriate mercy—in the right way.

18

More Beatitudes

The most difficult beatitude demands that we stop, think, and examine ourselves. "Blessed are the pure in heart."

The word *pure* originally meant "clean," and could be said of soiled clothes which have been washed clean.

Pure was regularly used for an army which was purged of all the discontented, cowardly, unwilling, and inefficient soldiers. The pure army was composed only of first-class soldiers.

The word appears commonly in the Greek language to describe milk or wine which is unadulterated with water, or metal which has no tinge of alloy.

To be "pure in heart" is to be unadulterated and unalloyed. Purity of heart is the road to blessedness—and the way of gladness.

149

LET YOUR MOTIVES
BE UNMIXED

"Blessed is the man whose motives are always unmixed, for that man shall see God." The beatitude of purity could read that way, for seldom indeed are even our finest motives unmixed. If we have given generously and liberally to some good cause, it may be that in the depths of our heart lingers some contentment in basking in the sunshine of our own self-approval. We may desire pleasure, praise, thanks, and credit. We may hope that people will see something heroic in us. Even a preacher is not free from the danger of self-satisfaction after preaching a good sermon.

It was the writer John Bunyan who was once told he had preached well on a Sunday, and he replied sadly, "The devil already told me that as I was coming down the pulpit steps."

Is our religion a thing in which we are conscious of nothing so much as the need of God within our hearts? Or is it a thing which gives us comfortable thoughts of our own piety? To examine our motives is a daunting and shameful thing, for there is little in this world that even the best of us do with completely unmixed motives.

LIFE'S BEST GOAL . . .
TO 'SEE' GOD

To see God . . . that privilege is reserved only for the pure in heart. It is one of the simple facts of life that we see only what we are able to see. The ordinary person goes out in a night filled with stars and sees only pinpoints of lights in the sky. But the astronomer will call the stars by name and move amongst them as a friend. The navigator will find in that same sky the means to bring his ship across the trackless seas to the desired haven.

In the sphere of life we see what we are able to see. A person with no knowledge cannot tell the painting of a great master from a worthless rag. People with filthy minds can see in any situation the material for soiled jest and ugly jokes. We reflect what we are by what we are able to see.

Those who seek perfectly pure motives will, by that seeking, refine their ability to see. By God's grace we keep our heart clean, or by lust we soil it. As we seek purity of heart we discover the path toward God. With the eyes of faith we see Him in the here and now, in people, in children, on the painted wing of a butterfly. We understand that God created it all, and we enter into the blessing of living in His presence.

BLESSED ARE THE PEACEMAKERS

Peace is more than the absence of trouble. It is everything which makes for our highest good. In the Bible, peace means the enjoyment of all good. The blessing promised to the peacemakers is not to those who merely "enjoy" peace, but to those who "make" it.

Often a peace lover can love peace in the wrong way. That person makes trouble and not peace by allowing threatening situations to develop. For peace's sake, he does not want to take any action.

The peace Jesus promises comes to those who do not evade the issues but face them, deal with them, conquer them. Peacemaking is not passive acceptance because we are afraid. It is actively facing trouble and *making* peace, even when the way of peace lies through struggle.

MAKE THIS WORLD A
BETTER PLACE . . .

Blessed are all those who make this world a better place to live. Abraham Lincoln said once, "Die when I may, I would like it to be said of me that I always pulled up a weed and planted a flower when I thought a flower would grow."

In every one of us lies a conflict between good and evil. We are tugged in two directions at once. I think of the poem,

> There are two natures in my breast,
> One is foul. One is blessed.
> One I love. One I hate.
> The one I feed will dominate.

Our highest task is to feed the motives which will bring peace and right relationships between man and man. Thank God there are people in whose presence bitterness cannot live—people who bridge the gulf, heal the breaches, sweeten the bitterness. Such people are doing God's work, for it is the great purpose of God to bring peace among all people.

Oh, the blessedness of that one who produces right relationships, for that one is doing God's work.

BLESSED ARE THOSE WHO ARE PERSECUTED FOR CHRIST'S SAKE

"Blessed are they who are persecuted for righteousness' sake; for theirs is the kingdom of heaven."

One of the outstanding qualities of Jesus Christ was His sheer honesty. He never left any doubt about what would happen to those who chose to follow Him. He made it clear that He had not come to make life easy, but to make men great. It is hard for us to imagine what those first Christians had to suffer. There was hardly a job in which a man might not be challenged for his loyalty to Christ. If it came to loyalty and making a living, the real Christian never hesitated to choose loyalty.

Loyalty to Christ disrupted work, social life, and even homelife. Often when someone became a Christian, other family members did not. It was literally true that a person might have to love Christ more than father and mother, husband or wife, brother and sister. Christianity involved a choice between all that was nearest and dearest.

The ancient bishop Polycarp of Smyrna was dragged by a mob before the tribunal and asked to sacrifice to Caesar. He said, "Eighty and six years I have served Christ and He has done me no wrong. How can I blaspheme my King Who saved me?" Polycarp was sentenced to die.

We have never had to suffer like that. And yet, the moment when Christianity seems likely to cost us something is the moment when we are open to demonstrate our love for Jesus Christ and our loyalty to Him in a way that all can see.

IN PERSECUTION,
WE ARE NOT ALONE

When we are challenged for our faith, we are not alone. If we are called upon to bear material loss, lose friends, suffer slander for the love of our principles, Christ will be near.

Why must we suffer? Because the church is called to be the conscience of the nation and of society. Others will want to silence the troublesome voice of conscience. It is not the duty of the Christian to criticize and condemn, but it may be that our every action is a silent condemnation of the unchristian motives of others. Ridicule awaits those who do not conform to the world's ways. Insults await those who insist on honor. Pressure may come to those who insist on doing an honest day's work in the name of Christ.

Christ calls us today not so much to die for Him as to live for Him. The Christian struggle and the call to glory come together.

"Blessed are you when men persecute you and say all manner of evil against you falsely, for my sake."

BE SALT AND LIGHT

Salt preserves from corruption. It gives life to food in the same way that Christ lends flavor to life. We bring to life the purity, antiseptic power, and the radiance that comes from knowing Christ. We are called to be "the salt of the earth."

A light is meant to be seen. Jesus warned us not to put our light of faith under a bushel basket. "Put the light on a lampstand," He said. There is no such thing as secret discipleship, for the secrecy destroys the discipleship, or the discipleship destroys the secrecy.

Our Christianity must be visible in the way we treat people, in the way we speak, in the way we live. There are people waiting for us to take the lead, to take a stand, to do things they themselves do not dare to do. We are called to be a guiding light.

Jesus said, "If I be lifted up from among men, I will draw all men unto Me." If only we can live so that He might be lifted up among us!

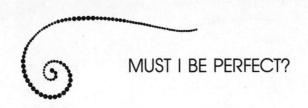

MUST I BE PERFECT?

Jesus said, "Be ye perfect." The original word for *perfect* meant "having a goal or a purpose." The word refers to growth. As we grow, we learn to love our enemies. That kind of love is a matter of the will. Jesus abolishes the old law of vengeance and introduces the new spirit of nonresentment and nonretaliation. In the stories about walking two miles with the person who compels you to walk one mile, or turning the other cheek only to be struck twice, He is introducing a higher law: "Even if a person directs at you the most deadly and calculating insult, you must on no account retaliate and you must on no account resent it."

When Lord Shaftesbury of England undertook the cause of the poor and the oppressed, he was warned that it would mean he would become unpopular with his friends and the people of his own class, and that he would have to give up all hope of being a cabinet minister. When he began his campaign to free the slaves, the slanderous rumor arose that he was a cruel husband, a wife-beater, and that he was secretly married to a black slave. Time and again he was excluded from some honor due to him. But he learned to overlook the insults. He learned never to retaliate, and he accomplished for peace and justice what many never have dared to try.

The Christian thinks not of rights, but of duties. Not of privileges, but of responsibilities. The Christian has learned—at all costs—to "love thy neighbor as thyself." The school of commitment teaches us to "be perfect, as our heavenly Father is perfect."

God is not interested in making us examples in His museum of perfection—but usable people in the world in which we live.

FOUR KINDS OF LOVE

As we become a new person in Christ, we experience the whole range of love, from the everyday love of family and friends to the highest love of all—unconditional love. Love comes in at least four forms:

The basic love is *family love*—love of a parent for a child and a child for a parent.

Next comes *eros,* the love of a man for a woman. The longing of this kind of love is not essentially bad, but contains the natural passion of human love. Historically, as time went on this kind of love began to be viewed as lust rather than love. Yet it is the natural love of a "man for a maid."

Friendship love is *philia.* This is the warmest and best Greek word for love. It describes real love and real affection. The word describes a person's dearest and truest friends and stands for the warmest and highest kind of respect and love.

Finally we have *agape.* This Greek word for love means unconquerable benevolence and invincible good will. If we regard a person with *agape,* it means that no matter what that person does to us, no matter how we are treated, insulted, injured, or grieved, we will never allow any bitterness to invade our hearts. We will guard that unconquerable benevolence and good will and seek nothing but that person's highest good.

Agape love does not mean the feeling of the heart which we cannot help, when it comes unbidden and unsought. It means a determination of the mind, whereby we achieve this unconquerable good will, even for those who hurt and injure us.

Jesus laid down this love as a basis for personal relationships. Only the grace of Christ can enable us to have such unconquerable benevolence and invincible good will. He makes possible this kind of love because the greatest characteristic of God is to love. The one thing that makes us more like Jesus is that we develop a love which never ceases to care for people, that learns to forgive as God forgives, and that loves others as He loves us.

"Love is not love which alters when it alteration finds."

—SHAKESPEARE

SEEK NO REWARD

He who is in love is always in debt. The last thing that enters his mind is that he has earned a reward. If a person has a legal view of life, he thinks in constant terms of the reward he has won. If a person has a loving view of life, the day of reward never occurs to him.

The great paradox of Christian reward is that the person who looks for reward and calculates it does not receive it. The person whose only motive is love (and who never thinks that he deserves a reward) does in fact receive it.

The rewards of the Christian life only seem like rewards to the spiritual person. First there is satisfaction—the sense of doing the right thing in obedience to Jesus Christ. Whatever else that doing may or may not bring, no one is ever disappointed in Jesus. No money can buy Christian satisfaction.

The second reward is more work to do. The world's reward is ease. The reward of the Christian is that God lays out more and more to do, with an even greater reward of satisfaction.

The third reward is what many have called "the vision of God." If goodness and rightness of relationships have been our quest all our days, then God is no stranger. All of life has been a drawing closer and closer to Him. In the end we pass into God's nearer presence without fear and with the radiant joy that is the greatest reward of all.

19

Commitment to Excellence

YOUR LIFE IS A WHEEL

Our life is circular.

In her book, *Gift from the Sea,* Anne Lindbergh used the symbol of a wheel to describe her life. In our lives, many forces pressure us—home, family, children, husband, church, work, committees, civic duties. As these forces pull at our perfectly rounded wheel, we must have a hub at the center that is strong and pure.

Unless our relationship with God is strong and central in our lives, our wheel will be "whomperjawed" in one of several directions. The rim can lose its perfect circularity and the wheel cannot turn smoothly.

If Jesus Christ holds all the spokes of our life together at the center of our wheel, we can be what He calls us to be.

THE ELEGANCE OF MOTHERING

Children are the priceless ingredients that make a home a potential powerhouse. A woman who knows the elegance of mothering and helping her children is inestimable in value. When she helps a child—whether it is hers or someone else's—the love and influence she shares helps humanity with an immediacy no other help given to human creatures in any stage of life can possibly give again.

Woman is innately gifted and equipped to comprehend life's meaning, and her home is love's locale on earth— her influence is limitless. Here is a poem that describes what I mean:

A WOMAN'S PLACE

They speak of a Woman's place
as though it had a limit—

There's not a place in earth or heaven,
There's not a task to mankind given,
There's not a blessing or a woe,
There's not a whispered "yes" or "no,"
There's not a life or death or birth,
That has a feather's weight of worth—

Without a woman in it.

KEEP YOUR COMMITMENT
TO EXCELLENCE ALIVE

Whatever our calling, we can take with us a commitment to excellence. It can make our homes a beautiful place, a place where love is communicated. Everything in life tends to tarnish. Silver has to be polished. Chrome has to be rubbed to keep it clean. Brass must be polished. Gold must be polished to remove the accumulation of particles from the air. Human relationships, most of all, must be carefully cared for.

Tom Landry said once, "The ultimate in life is not in achieving and winning, but in giving God first priority." Most of all, we have to continually call on God and talk to Him, cultivating that primary relationship with our Creator above all else.

Commitment to excellence starts with the very first thing in the morning—every day—getting plugged into the source of all excellence, all power, all resources. I am called to live in perfect relation to God. Then my life will produce a longing after God when I am with others.

MAKE A COMMITMENT
TO YOUR GOAL

Do you have a goal? If so, you must have a commitment to it. That goal must be to seek for excellence in everything you do. And your goal must never be vague.

In fact, remember to have a set of specific goals—emotional, spiritual, physical, financial. Set them. Put a timetable on them. Then reach for them. You will be amazed at what you can accomplish.

I met a man recently and asked him, "How are you?" He replied, "Pretty good, under the circumstances."

I asked him, "What in the world are you doing *under* the circumstances? Get *over* those circumstances." With carefully chosen goals and a commitment to attain them, we can discover the very best in the circumstances that are ours each day.

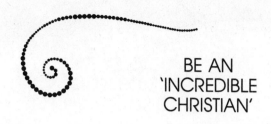

BE AN 'INCREDIBLE CHRISTIAN'

I wrote in my Bible, "Don't ever be afraid of tomorrow. God is already there." When we get hold of what it cost God to justify us, and the love that made Him do it, we discover that the freedom of our personal worth is bound up in His character. He believed that I was worth dying for. He declared that those who believe are justified. And so, I am *somebody*!

In his book, *That Incredible Christian,* A. W. Tozer said, "In seeking to know God better, we must bear firmly in mind that we need not try to persuade God. He is already persuaded in our favor, not by our prayers, but by the generous goodness of His own heart. It is God's nature to give Himself to every virtuous soul."

The incredible Christian loses her life, to save it. She is strongest when she is weakest. She fears God but is not afraid of Him. She knows that only in Christ can she become her whole self.

That wonderful martyred missionary, Jim Elliott, was told that he was a fool to go to the Auca Indians in the jungles of South America. He replied, "No man is a fool to lose that which he cannot keep to gain that which he cannot lose."

When we deeply desire a commitment to excellence—in our relationship with God, with home, and with others—we will discover the blessedness of the "incredible Christian."

LIVE BY
THE PEACE OF GOD, NOT
THE PRESSURES OF LIFE

We must learn to say, "God, help me to live by the peace of God, instead of by the pressures of life."
Perhaps our prayer could be:

> Our Father, we know that each day we must make decisions. By our choices we determine what we are.
> May our judgments be made not simply for our own convenience, or to suit a passing fancy, but with the purpose of doing that which is acceptable in Your sight—that which is truly excellent.
> Keep us from going astray. May we say with the words of Psalm 73: 23–26, "You, O God, will keep on guiding me all of my life with your wisdom and your counsel."
> Amen.

As one writer reminds us, the quest for excellence is "the hardest battle any human can fight"—to be yourself "in a world which is doing its best . . . to make you everybody else."

Let's never stop aiming for the highest form of excellence—a life lived in accordance with the peace of God!

Epilogue

When this book was being finished, I had a time to review and renew my spiritual walk with my Lord—I had surgery to remove a small tumor under my ear. Expecting a minor surgery, I was shocked to be told the tumor contained rare cancer cells. Now, six weeks later, I have had a series of radium treatments—five external and four days of radium implants in my face and neck. The left side of my face suffered temporary nerve damage during the surgery, and I've learned how special it is for one's eye to blink naturally. Truly I can say with the psalmist, "We are fearfully and wonderfully made." I'm now on the road to recovery, but I've learned once again what the words of one of Grace Noll Crowell's poems mean. May they bless you, too, when you are tired.

FOR ONE WHO IS TIRED

Dear Child,
God does not say today, "Be strong"—
   He knows your strength is spent—
   He knows how long the road has been—

How weary you've become, for
He who walked this earth alone—
  Each boggy lowland and each rugged hill,
    understands—
  And so He simply says, "Be still,
  Be still and know that I am God."
The hour is late and you must rest awhile,—
  And you must wait
Until life's empty reservoirs fill up
  As slow rain fills an empty upturned cup.
Hold up your cup, dear child, for God to fill.
  He only asks that you be still.

Everlastingly in His care,
Mary C. Crowley